FRESH IDEAS IN
Promotion

LYNN HALLER

NORTH LIGHT BOOKS

Cincinnati, Ohio

Acknowledgments

I'd like to acknowledge the team of talented people who cheerfully (I think) and conscientiously (I know) put this project together: Terri Boemker, whose eagle eye ensured that the art would be sized correctly and that the text would be typo-free; Brian Roeth, who came up with a great, flexible design for the book's interior; Julie Wilson, who helped me deal with the mass quantity of art that was shipped to my office, as well as helping me set up for the judging; Angela Lennert, who did a great job designing the cover; Melissa Wingham, who dummied the book intelligently (no pun intended); Perri Weinberg-Schenker, who copyedited the manuscript; Pam Monfort, who shot all the pieces for which we didn't have slides; and our in-house team of judges—David Lewis, Clare Finney, Brian Roeth, Libby Fellerhoff, and Bryn Mooth—who took time out of their busy schedules to help me decide who would be in this book. Thanks to all for making this book such fun to put together.

I'd also like to acknowledge the efforts of the office managers and other support personnel within the studios included here, who entered this work for our consideration, and who made sure we got the art and information we needed. And of course, this book couldn't exist without the talented designers, illustrators and photographers who have shared their work with us here; ultimately, this book belongs to them.

Fresh Ideas in Promotion. Copyright © 1994 by North Light Books.

Printed and bound in China. All rights reserved. No part of this book may be reproduced in any form or by any electronic or mechanical means including information storage and retrieval systems without permission in writing from the publisher, except by a reviewer, who may quote brief passages in a review. Published by North Light Books, an imprint of F&W Publications, Inc., 1507 Dana Avenue, Cincinnati, Ohio 45207. (800) 289-0963. First edition.

This hardcover edition of *Fresh Ideas in Promotion* features a "self-jacket" that eliminates the need for a separate dust jacket. It provides sturdy protection for your book while it saves paper, trees and energy.

Other fine North Light Books are available from your local bookstore, or direct from the publisher.

98 97 96 95   5 4 3 2

Library of Congress Cataloging-in-Publication Data

Fresh ideas in promotion /[edited by] Lynn Haller.
     p.   cm.
    Includes index.
    ISBN 0-89134-620-1
    1. Commercial art—United States—Themes, motives.   I. Haller,
Lynn.
    NC998.5.A1F74 1994
    741.6'0973—dc20   94-12062
                                     CIP

Interior design by Brian Roeth
Cover design by Angela Lennert
The copyright notices and photography credits on page 136 constitute an extension of this copyright page.

METRIC CONVERSION CHART		
TO CONVERT	**TO**	**MULTIPLY BY**
Inches	Centimeters	2.54
Centimeters	Inches	0.4
Feet	Centimeters	30.5
Centimeters	Feet	0.03
Yards	Meters	0.9
Meters	Yards	1.1
Sq. Inches	Sq. Centimeters	6.45
Sq. Centimeters	Sq. Inches	0.16
Sq. Feet	Sq. Meters	0.09
Sq. Meters	Sq. Feet	10.8
Sq. Yards	Sq. Meters	0.8
Sq. Meters	Sq. Yards	1.2
Pounds	Kilograms	0.45
Kilograms	Pounds	2.2
Ounces	Grams	28.4
Grams	Ounces	0.04

I n a nation where every potential consumer—and that means everybody over the age of three—is subject to a never-ending barrage of promotional material, what constitutes a "fresh idea in promotion"? Does such a thing exist anymore? And even if it does, can designers of modest printed pieces—in this world of twenty-four-hour shopping networks and million-dollar ad campaigns—cut through this visual clutter and get their own promotions noticed?

The examples in this book demonstrate that, indeed, plenty of designers are still finding fresh and creative ways to promote themselves and their clients. How do these pieces qualify as "fresh ideas"? Some utilize an original and attention-getting format; others incorporate an innovative solution to an old design problem.

While the promotions in this book come in every format, promote every type of client, and have budgets ranging from tight to great, they do have something in common: The designers of each piece clearly considered the following key questions. Ask yourself these questions when trying to come up with fresh promotional ideas, and let your answers lead you to your own winning promotions.

• What is the piece's message? And what's the best way for this piece to communicate this message to its audience? No doubt, you'll have more luck selling investments to a Fortune 500 type with a conservative glossy brochure than with a day-glo jack-in-the-box promotion. On the other hand, do keep in mind that designs that take a calculated risk are more likely to get noticed. So if you have a concept that you think is worth gambling on, consider an approach that bucks the trends. For instance, see the ASTech campaign on page 69 and the National Air and Space Museum piece on page 71 for examples of promotions that effectively used a nontraditional approach to get the attention of a conservative, moneyed audience.

• What is the competition doing? Is there a valid reason for this—for instance, non-profit events are usually promoted with posters because they're effective and cheap—or is it simply an approach that has been overused? Some of the promotions in this book utilize formats that customarily promote other types of products, such as postcards being used to promote furniture or an academic conference (see pages 106 and 79). Others employ an original format that's fun to get, and hard to throw out (see the playing card portfolio on page 97).

When you're planning your next promotional or self-promotional piece, think through all your choices for two-dimensional or three-dimensional pieces. Would a quarterly newsletter be a more effective use of your promotional budget than a one-shot spiral-bound booklet? Should you use a postcard or a multi-panel brochure mailed in an envelope? Can a nonprofit event be promoted with a T-shirt, a poster or both? Which format will stand out from the crowd? What will get your audience's attention?

• How can I get the most out of my (limited) budget? This book includes examples of designers who spent time rather than money on their pieces by hand-binding or hand-coloring them. Or they used a little production savvy to stretch their limited funds—for instance, by batching more than one piece on the same press run, or by using a limited number of inks wisely. Still other designers came up with campaigns for a client in exchange for a credit on the piece; with this simple tactic, they got their names out to people who might never have heard of them without incurring the cost of the piece's production or distribution.

• Finally, on a more basic level, what is your design philosophy? Do you consider your own or your studio's design style to be an essential part of a piece's end message, or do you think your style should bend—or even change radically—to communicate the client's message? This is a particularly crucial point for beginning designers to ponder—if it's important to you to attract clients who specifically want your style, you need to make sure you're clearly communicating this style in your own self-promotional pieces. But if you want potential clients to know how well you can communicate a wide variety of messages, be sure to convey that too in your self-promotional pieces. Before designing promotional material for clients, you'll need to decide where you stand on this issue, and make sure you communicate this to your client early in your relationship.

This, obviously, is just a start—only you know what kind of audience you're trying to reach, what your local market is like, what your production limitations are, and what your client needs to communicate. The pieces included in this book—the top 20 percent of the entries we received—should thus not be thought of as examples to copy, but instead as inspiration that "fresh ideas in promotion" still do exist—and that they can exist no matter what your client or your budget.

SELF-PROMOTIONAL PIECES
FOR DESIGNERS

Art Director/Studio Michael Strassburger/Modern Dog
Designers/Studio Michael Strassburger, Robynne Raye, Vittorio Costarella/Modern Dog
Photographer Rex Rystedt (Modern Dog staff photo)
Client/Service Modern Dog, Seattle, WA/graphic design
Paper Cardboard, bond paper
Colors One, black
Type Helvetica
Printing Laser printing (fake newspaper liner)
Software Aldus PageMaker

Initial Print Run 25
Cost $2,000

Concept Playing off their design firm's name, the designers of this piece came up with a promotion that even the most jaded art director could not forget or want to throw away. Inspired by a pink fur box they received as a thank you from their colleague Frank Zepponi, this box—covered with synthetic dog fur and bound by a leather collar—can be filled with any work samples appropriate for

its recipient. This playful promotion conveys the personality of the studio, ensuring that Modern Dog will attract the kind of clients it wants to work with.
Special Visual Effects The box is lined with a mocked-up newspaper lining—output on a laser printer by Modern Dog—that follows through the dog concept; every number listed in these classifieds is the phone or fax number of Modern Dog. Its address and phone number are also engraved on the dog tag that tops off the piece.

Distribution of Piece An initial twenty-five pieces were distributed via UPS to potential clients in the entertainment industry.
Response to Promotion This piece generated great publicity for Modern Dog, resulting in interviews and articles about the studio in trade magazines; this in turn led to multiple speaking engagements for the principals. In addition, more than $40,000 in revenue can be directly linked to the box.

Art Director/Studio Orly Zeewy/Zeewy Design

Designers/Studio Orly Zeewy, Lia Calhoun/Zeewy Design

Copywriter Jane Palmer

Photographer John Carlano

Client/Service Zeewy Design, Narberth, PA/graphic design

Paper Gilbert ESSE (cover, text), Osprey Royal Gloss (inserts)

Colors Four, black and match (booklet), and four, process (inserts)

Type Galliard, Univers Extra Black Extended, Fenice

Printing Offset

Software QuarkXPress, Aldus FreeHand

Initial Print Run 500

Cost $5,000

Concept This self-promotional booklet effectively communicates Zeewy Design's marketing and design expertise. The interior of the booklet itself is plain text, uncluttered with visuals and printed on a textured, uncoated paper stock; the simplicity of this presentation focuses attention on the booklet's message and gives credibility to its content. Within the inside back cover, four-color inserts depict actual projects designed by the studio; the front is a photograph of the project, and the back contains a short explanation of it. This format allows the studio to customize the booklet for individual clients. The overall effect is contemporary but classic, a reflection of the tastes of the clientele the studio has targeted.

Cost-Saving Techniques The material included in the booklet itself is timeless; the client list and project samples are printed as inserts and can be changed as needed without reprinting the whole piece.

Distribution of Piece The piece was used as a leave-behind, as well as being mailed to a small group from a list of new, existing and potential clients.

Response to Promotion In the first three months of use, the brochure has been instrumental in increasing new business by more than 50 percent.

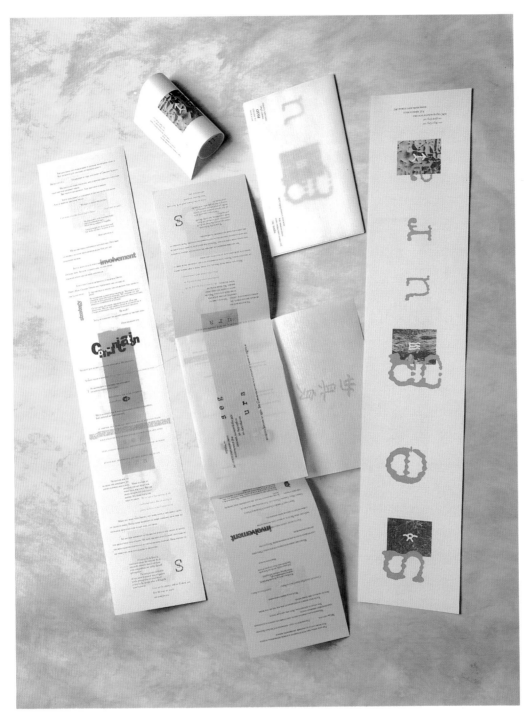

Art Director/Studio Carlos Segura/Segura Inc.
Designer/Studio Carlos Segura/Segura Inc.
Photographer Steve Nozicka
Client/Service Segura Inc., Chicago, IL/graphic design
Paper Gilbert ESSE White
Colors Two, black and match
Type Albertan, typewriter
Printing Offset
Software QuarkXPress, Adobe Photoshop, Adobe Illustrator
Initial Print Run 2,000

Concept While using a traditional format—a brochure—to promote its studio, Segura Inc. makes this old idea fresh by utilizing an unexpected layout, layers of semitransparent paper stock, and a cutting-edge type treatment. Effective use of white space breaks up the large block of conceptual copy included in the brochure and makes it less intimidating to recipients.
Special Visual Effect A fragment of the firm's name, printed the length of the brochure's exterior, shows through the envelope, giving the unopened piece intrigue.
Cost-Saving Technique Two-color printing kept costs down.
Distribution of Piece The piece was mailed to new businesses in the area.

STEWART MONDERER
DESIGN, INC.

Art Director/Studio Stewart Monderer/Stewart Monderer Design, Inc.

Designers/Studio Stewart Monderer, Robert Davison, Kathleen Smith/Stewart Monderer Design, Inc.

Client/Service Stewart Monderer Design, Inc., Boston, MA/graphic design

Paper Tuscan Terra (cover), Gleneagle Dull (text)

Colors Two, match, and four, process

Type Franklin Gothic, Garamond #3

Printing Offset

Software QuarkXPress

Initial Print Run 4,000

Cost $20,000

Concept This four-by-nine-inch booklet enables the design firm to introduce its capabilities to poten-

tial clients without having to show its portfolio or part with rare printed samples. Copy accompanying each project communicates individual project objectives.

Special Production Technique The entire brochure was prepared on the computer; mechanicals were not necessary.

Cost-Saving Technique The brochure was sized to fit into a cost-effective #10 envelope.

Distribution of Piece The piece was distributed by mail or in person on an as-needed basis to current and potential clients.

Response to Promotion The promotion generated calls to see the firm's portfolio, as well as invitations to bid on projects; it also gained the firm visibility and recognition.

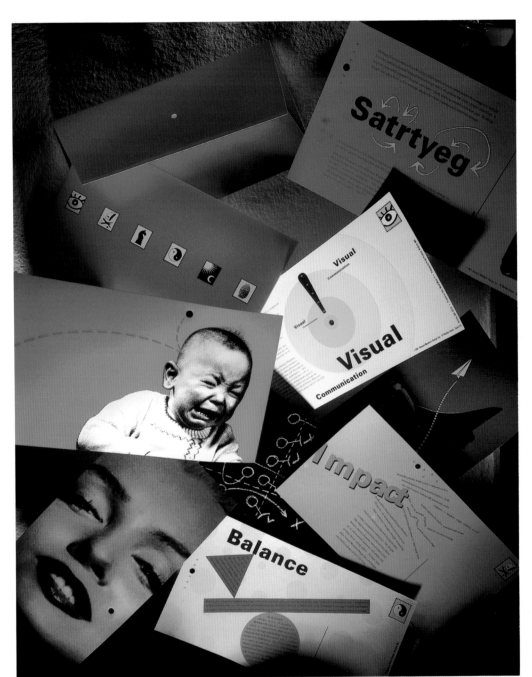

STEWART MONDERER DESIGN, INC.

Art Director/Studio Stewart Monderer/Stewart Monderer Design, Inc.
Designers/Studio Stewart Monderer, Robert Davison, Jane Winsor/Stewart Monderer Design, Inc.
Illustrator Richard Goldberg
Client/Service Stewart Monderer Design, Inc., Boston, MA/graphic design
Paper Mead Mark I (postcards), Mead Moistrite Matte (envelope)
Colors Four, match, and four, process
Type Garamond 3, Univers
Printing Offset
Software Aldus FreeHand, Aldus PageMaker
Initial Print Run 21,500
Cost $23,000

Concept This series of six over-sized postcards was designed to illustrate some of the distinctive qualities Stewart Monderer Design, Inc., uses to transform concepts into powerful visual communications. The front of each postcard visually presents a theme; the back spells out the concept and then follows up with brief copy explaining it. Themes include contrast, individuality, balance, strategy, impact and visual communication.

Special Visual Effects Each postcard is die-cut to mark its place in the sequence. The various small icons used to mark where the stamp goes further carry out the concept of the postcard.

Cost-Saving Technique Mead Paper donated paper and most of the printing costs in exchange for 20,000 copies for use as a commercial sample.

Distribution of Piece A postcard was sent out in sequence every two weeks to existing and potential clients.

Response to Promotion Because of Mead's use of the paper as a sample, it generated national exposure for the studio. It generated interest from clients as well.

STUDIO WILKS

Art Director/Studio Richard Wilks/Studio Wilks

Designer/Studio Teri Wilks/Studio Wilks

Client/Service Studio Wilks, Los Angeles, CA/graphic design

Paper Wyndstone Waffle, Wyndstone Marble

Colors One, black

Type Bank Gothic

Printing Laser, offset

Software Aldus FreeHand

Initial Print Run 350

Cost $2,500

Concept The piece's miniportfolio format enables this design firm to target its promotion to each potential client. Each version features seven examples of the studio's work (out of a pool of fourteen used in this promotion) targeted specifically to that client's design needs. The cover of the portfolio is Wyndstone Waffle, a uniquely textured paper, and the self-mailer that wraps around the piece is this same paper, fastened with Velcro. These details give the piece sophistication, as well as the element of surprise.

Cost-Saving Technique Color copies rather than four-color printing were used for the interior images.

Distribution of Piece The piece has been mailed or personally given to potential clients on an as-needed basis.

Art Director/Studio Laura Christensen/Pace Studios, Inc.

Creative Director/Studio Joel Blum/Pace Studios, Inc.

Designer/Studio Laura Christensen/Pace Studios, Inc.

Photographer Ed Carey

Client/Service Pace Studios, Inc., San Francisco, CA/graphic design

Paper Curtis Parchment (flyleaf), Consolidated Papers Reflections (cover, text)

Colors One, match, and four, process, plus varnish

Type Coronet (introduction); Garamond, Bodoni, custom faces (text); Roman Shaded (credits)

Printing Offset

Software Adobe Photoshop, QuarkXPress

Initial Print Run 10,000

Concept Inspired by the art director's visit to the archives of San Francisco's historic Ghirardelli Company—archives that had never been seen by the general public—this promotion was designed to bring these treasures to light, as well as to serve as a lavish joint promotion for all involved.

Special Visual Effects A special match gold metallic ink gives the booklet a subtly luxurious look; the spot dull-tinted varnish on the interior pictures alone (leaving most of the text without varnish) gives the photographs added luster.

Special Production Technique Layouts were done on the computer and color proofs pulled to finalize everything before going to typesetting and separations.

Cost-Saving Technique Photographer Ed Carey, color separator Hollis Digital Imaging, printer Imperial Litho, food stylist Sandra Cook, and prop stylist Carol Hacker all donated their services in exchange for being credited in the booklet.

Distribution of Piece The piece was distributed twice: once on Valentine's Day by Pace Studios, and once as a promotion by Consolidated Papers.

Response to Promotion The studio landed one new account and received nationwide recognition from paper merchants; the piece also earned two national design awards, which gave the studio a higher profile.

JAGER DIPAOLA
KEMP DESIGN

Creative Director/Studio
Michael Jager/Jager DiPaola Kemp
Design

Art Directors/Studio Giovanna
Jager ("Shoes"), David Covell
("AIDS"), Janet Johnson
("Flux")/Jager DiPaola Kemp
Design

Designers/Studio Giovanna
Jager ("Shoes"); David Covell
("AIDS"); Dan Sharp, Steve
Bowman ("Flux")/Jager DiPaola
Kemp Design

Client/Service Jager DiPaola
Kemp Design, Burlington,
VT/graphic design

Paper Various

Colors Various

Type Various

Printing Silkscreen

Initial Print Run 150 each

Concept Jager DiPaola Kemp
Design instituted this bimonthly
"Why Design?" poster series as a
way to communicate the power of
design to clients, both through the
visual impact of the posters themselves and through the copy's conceptual content. Each poster in the
series comes with a vellum overlay
containing thoughtful commentary
about the value of design, as well
as information about the studio
itself; this keeps the posters themselves uncluttered with copy. Since
the posters can be viewed with or
without the vellum overlay, each
poster's visual message is doubled.
Each poster is also a bimonthly calendar; the studio encourages
clients to crop off the calendar portion once the time has elapsed and
frame the posters.

Distribution of Piece The piece
is mailed and hand-delivered to
clients and prospective clients.

Response to Promotion Verbal
response has been positive, and a
number of clients have hung up
one or more of the posters.

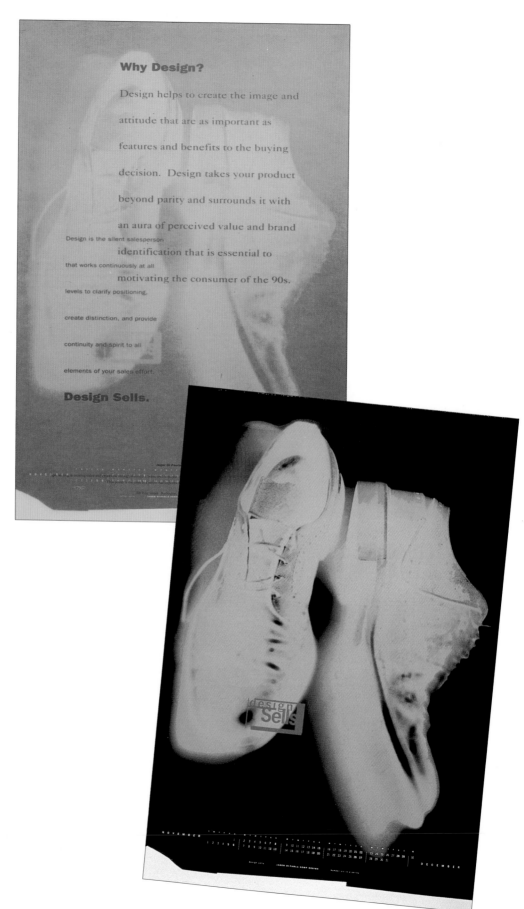

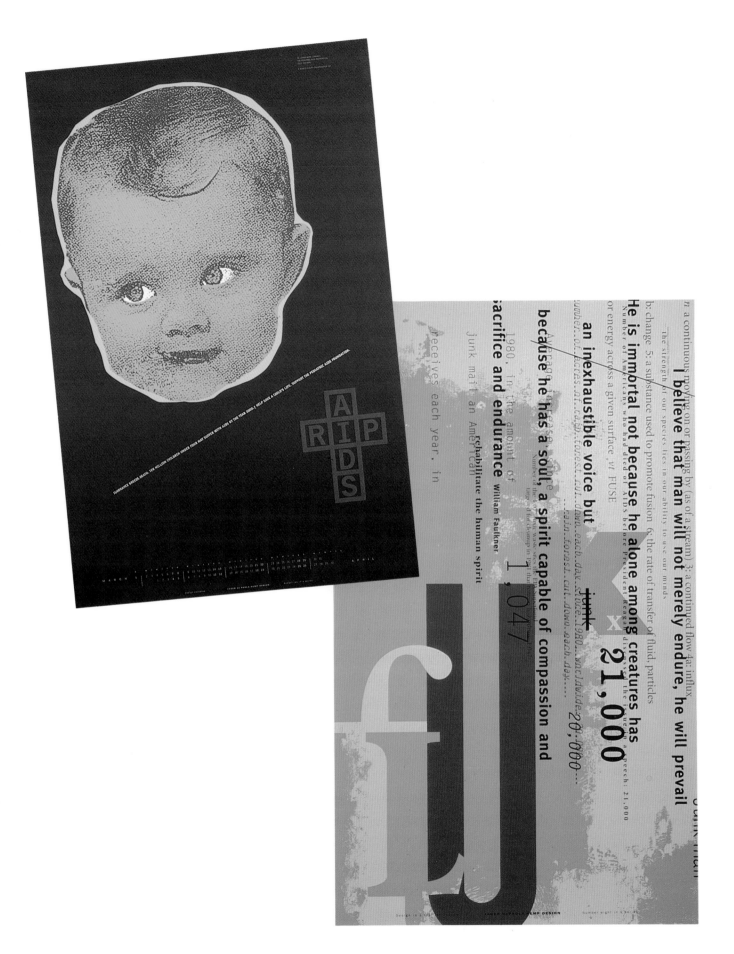

CLEMENT MOK DESIGNS, INC.

Art Directors/Studio Clement Mok, Doris Mitsch/Clement Mok designs, Inc.

Designer/Studio Vic Zauderer/ Clement Mok designs, Inc.

Client/Service Clement Mok designs, Inc., San Francisco, CA/graphic design

Paper EverGreen Spruce Cover, EverGreen Almond Text, Mohawk Matte

Colors One, match, and four, process

Type Garamond 3 Old Style

Printing Offset

Software QuarkXPress, Adobe Illustrator, Adobe Photoshop

Initial Print Run 5,000

Cost $60,000

Concept This self-promotional booklet reaches beyond the usual miniportfolio of a studio's work or statement of its philosophy to focus on the clients' needs, and how Clement Mok designs, Inc., has addressed them in past projects. After some introductory background about the studio, the booklet is divided into five detailed case studies of projects by the studio. Copy explains what the clients' product and needs were. Since the studio specializes in corporate identity design for technologically complex products, this explanation is often necessary for the reader to understand why the final design solution worked so well for the product. Yet the booklet's oversized 8½-by-14-inch format still allows room for plenty of visuals, to help complete the story. This thoughtful booklet effectively appeals to its sophisticated audience.

Special Visual Effect The use of a classic, utilitarian design and muted colors focuses the reader on the booklet's content.

Special Production Technique The entire project—from design through electronic files to the printer—was composed digitally on

the Macintosh.

Distribution of Piece The piece was mailed monthly to directors of creative services in batches of fifty to one hundred.

Response to Promotion Verbal response from potential clients has been extremely positive.

Designers/Studio Kathryn Klein, James Skiles, Tim McGrath, Gorham Palmer/Midnight Oil Studios

Photographer Black Box

Illustrators James Skiles, Tim McGrath, Gorham Palmer

Client/Service Midnight Oil Studios/graphic design

Paper Champion Kromekote (poster), 92.5 Ikonofix Matte Cover (postcards)

Colors Six; four, process, plus match metallic and spot gloss varnish

Type Various

Printing Offset

Software Adobe Illustrator, Adobe Photoshop

Initial Print Run 2,500, each phase

Cost $30,000

Concept This "Work Ethics" self-promotional campaign fits in nicely with the Midnight Oil Studios name and style. The copy—on both the calendar poster and the cards—manages to convey the value of work in an entertaining, nonpreachy way. The set of twelve postcards features philosophical, yet slightly tongue-in-cheek, commentary about twelve different professions; a business reply postcard addressed to Midnight Oil is attached to the "designer" card.

Special Visual Effects The use of spot varnish gives texture to the outside of the card folder and the borders of the poster. The back of the poster features a white and yellow pattern of little workers with mallet and wrench in hand. Screen-tinted stock photography of people at work is used as a background pattern on both the card folder and on the poster.

Distribution of Piece The poster was either mailed or hand-delivered at the beginning of the year to current and potential clients; the cards were mailed in December of the same year.

Response to Promotion The pieces have brought lots of interest and work assignments.

SELF-PROMOTIONAL PIECES FOR ILLUSTRATORS AND PHOTOGRAPHERS

Designers/Studios Steve Gabor/Salvato & Coe Associates; Marcia Gabor/Conrad, Phillips & Vutech
Illustrator Greg Dearth
Clients/Services Scott Hull Associates, Dayton, OH/artists' representative; Beckett Paper, Hamilton, OH/paper mill
Paper Beckett Glacier White Concept Wove Cover
Colors Six, match, and four, process
Type Various
Printing Offset
Software Aldus FreeHand
Initial Print Run 50,000

Concept This promotion served a dual purpose: to show off some of Dearth's projects from the past year, and to showcase the use of various ink coverages on the Beckett paper used for the booklet. The "Get a Grip" theme, with its fly motif and pun-laden introductory copy, is playful and attention-getting.

Cost-Saving Techniques Scott Hull Associates and Beckett Paper teamed up for this promotion; Beckett traded paper for design and production, and the two companies printed the project jointly to keep costs down.

Distribution of Piece The piece was mailed by Scott Hull Associates and handed out by Beckett representatives throughout 1993 to art directors, creative directors and designers.

Response to Promotion The promotion resulted in an increase in calls for Dearth's services.

SCOTT HULL
ASSOCIATES

Designer/Studio Dawn Horn/
Littleton 2
Illustrators Mary Grandpré,
Franklin Hammond, David La
Fleur, Curtis Parker, Cheryl Cooper
Client/Service Scott Hull
Associates, Dayton, OH/artists' rep-
resentative
Paper Beckett Concept Wove
Cover
Colors Four, black and match
Type Various
Printing Offset
Software Aldus PageMaker
Initial Print Run 10,000

Concept This modest, inexpensive group of postcards supported
Scott Hull Associates' more elaborate "The World of Classic Idioms"
promotion, seen on page 17. The
postcards give the recipients a
taste of the work of five illustrators
featured in that promotion, and
direct them to request a copy of
the promotion if they want additional samples of these illustrators'
work. Each postcard features a single illustration on the front and
contact information on the back, in
case one of the pieces was separated from the rest.
Cost-Saving Technique The job
was run on the tail end of another
project to avoid paper waste.
Distribution of Piece The piece
was distributed in two mailings to
art directors, designers and editorial staff.
Response to Promotion The
promotion resulted in assignments
and calls requesting samples from
clients' files.

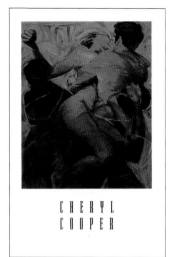

Art Directors/Studios Eric Rickabaugh/Rickabaugh Graphics; Scott Hull, Frank Sturges/Scott Hull Associates
Designer/Studio Eric Rickabaugh/Rickabaugh Graphics
Photographer George C. Anderson
Illustrators Various
Client/Service Scott Hull Associates, Dayton, OH/artists' representative
Paper Simpson Quest Text, Excellence Gloss Text
Colors Two, black and match (flysheets); one, black, and four,

process (text)
Type Bernhard Modern, Futura (text); Bodoni, Fenice (cover); Spire (introduction)
Printing Offset
Software Adobe Illustrator, Aldus PageMaker
Initial Print Run 12,000

Concept This booklet, the third in a series of promotions for Scott Hull Associates, revolves around the theme "The World of Classic Idioms." Copywriter Jeff Morris's fanciful origins of various idioms are visually interpreted by the

illustrators featured in the promotion. Each spread spotlights the work of a single illustrator, with the left-hand page featuring the visual interpretation of the idiom's origin, and the first page of the 4-inch flysheet being the humorous copy. The back of the flysheet presents a photo of and statement by the illustrator, and the right-hand side of the spread features other work by that illustrator.
Special Visual Effect The typographic treatment of each idiom visually interprets the idiom's meaning.

Cost-Saving Technique Rickabaugh Graphics provided design services at a discount in exchange for being included in the piece of promotional copy.
Distribution of Piece The piece was mailed throughout 1993 to agencies, design firms, publishers and corporations.
Response to Promotion The project gave Scott Hull Associates an identity in the market, and its recipients appreciated this idea-oriented promotion.

ROBB DEBENPORT

Art Director/Studio Bryan L. Peterson/Peterson & Company
Designer/Studio Bryan L. Peterson/Peterson & Company
Photographer Robb Debenport
Illustrator Bryan L. Peterson
Client/Service Robb Debenport, Dallas, TX/photography
Paper Mohawk Superfine (cover), Mohawk Superfine and Splendorlux (text)
Colors Four, process, plus varnish, and two, match
Type Teknik, Insignia, Fenice, Helvetica, Weiss, Goudy Old Style, Stuyvesant, Copperplate, Zurich, Humanist, Bauer Bodoni, Bernhard Modern, Futura Extra Bold
Printing Offset
Software QuarkXPress, Adobe Illustrator
Initial Print Run 22,000
Cost None (services and materials donated)

Concept This booklet uses quotations and corresponding images that are tied into basic photographic principles such as form, line and texture. The typographic treatment of each quotation provides a visual interpretation of its content. The whimsical way these components are connected draws viewers into the piece and gives it an interactive element.

Special Visual Effect A fragment of each typographic treatment used in the booklet is featured in collage format on the cover.

Special Production Techniques All photos for the piece were batched together on one sheet of Splendorlux; all text was batched on one sheet of Superfine and printed in two colors.

Cost-Saving Technique All materials and services were donated in exchange for credit and contact information on the last page of the booklet.

Distribution of Piece The piece was mailed and hand-distributed to designers, art directors and printers.

Response to Promotion Responses have been positive, and the photographer is solidly booked now.

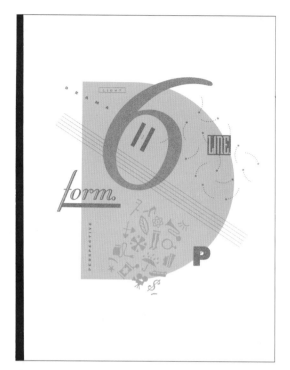

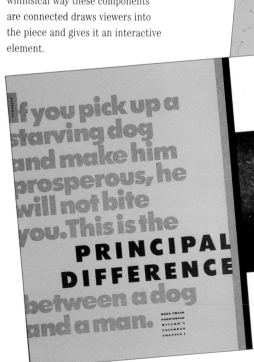

Art Director Stephen Alcorn
Designer Stephen Alcorn
Photographer Stephen Alcorn
Illustrator Stephen Alcorn
Client/Products Stephen Alcorn, Cambridge, NY/prints, paintings, portraits and illustration
Paper Mohawk Innovation Dull Coat, Champion Kromekote
Colors Four, process
Printing Offset

Concept This set of postcards—a promotion conceived by the artist's late father, designer John Alcorn—serves as an effective miniportfolio of the work of artist Stephen Alcorn. Whether sent individually, with a note from the artist, or as a packet to be used by the recipient, the postcard format gives the artist a way to display a wide variety of images and media in a single format. This format, associated as it is with fine art, also connotes artistic integrity.
Cost-Saving Technique Paper was donated by Mohawk Paper; Morgan Press donated printing and typesetting services.
Distribution of Piece The piece has been mailed at even intervals to designers and publishers around the world.
Response to Promotion The artist has received delighted responses from recipients (some even framed the postcards), as well as numerous illustration assignments.

PATRICK BARTA
PHOTOGRAPHY

Art Director/Studio Patrick
Barta/Patrick Barta Photography
Designer/Studio Don Faia/Faia
Design
Copywriter John Beezer
Photographer Patrick Barta
Client/Service Patrick Barta
Photography, Seattle, WA/commer-
cial photography
Paper Simpson EverGreen
Silvertip Cover
Colors Four, process ("Polaroid");
one, black (body)
Type Helvetica Narrow Regular,
Copperplate Gothic (Polaroid cover
copy); Avant Garde (logo)
Printing Offset
Initial Print Run 5,000
Cost $5,300

Concept This campaign of direct
mail pieces uses a mock Polaroid
test image format to involve recipients in the piece. The exterior
bears tongue-in-cheek, soft-sell
copy, along with the photographer's
logo and symbols for "no weddings,"
"no passports" and "no ego." The
interior consists of a single
"Polaroid," along with the photographer's name, address and phone
number. While the format throughout the campaign remains con-
stant, the copy and the image
change with each mailing.
Special Production Technique
Type for each piece was made into
a rubber stamp and hand-stamped.
Cost-Saving Techniques Pieces
were hand-assembled by the photographer and his staff to cut down
production costs. Design and layout was done on a trade-out basis
with Faia Design.
Distribution of Piece Mailings go
out every six to eight weeks.
Response to Promotion Three
projects have been generated as a
direct result of the campaign; the
photographer's name recognition
has also increased substantially.

Designer/Studio Ed Schweitzer/Fusion Design, Inc.
Photographer John Payne
Client/Service John Payne Photography, Ltd., Chicago, IL/photography
Paper Kraft Speckletone (cover), Hopper Proterra (body), Gilbert Gilclear Vellum
Colors Four, process, and two, match
Type Goudy (cover), Garamond Italic (interior)
Printing Offset
Software QuarkXPress
Initial Print Run 1,000
Cost $8,500

Concept This lovely four-by-five-inch booklet gives the recipient a feel for this photographer's range. The piece, with its small format and handmade feel, was designed to stand out from the usual glossy self-promotional piece. This booklet conveys quality and attention to detail—exactly right for a photographer.

Special Visual Effect The first page of each section is a single word or phrase on a white page; the second page of the spread is a vellum page with a brown-inked halftone, which layers intriguingly with the photograph underneath it.

Cost-Saving Technique Printing most of the body of the booklet on one side of the paper, then folding the paper over to give the effect of a heavier stock printed on both sides, gives this piece a unique feel while saving on printing costs.

Distribution of Piece The piece was mailed and handed out, both by the photographer and his representative, to art directors and designers.

Response to Promotion While this promotion has only been distributed for a few months, some art directors have already said that the booklet has convinced them to hire Payne.

Art Director/Studio Stephen Schudlich/Stephen Schudlich Illustration + Design

Designer/Studio Stephen Schudlich/Stephen Schudlich Illustration + Design

Illustrator Stephen Schudlich

Client/Service Stephen Schudlich Illustration + Design, Troy, MI/illustration and design

Paper Champion Kromekote mounted on chipboard (puzzle, Rolodex); Neenah UV Ultra II (insert card)

Colors Four, process

Type Linoscript, Futura Condensed, Helvetica Copperplate (puzzle); Agency Open Face, Copperplate (insert card); Helvetica, Agency Open Face, Linoscript (Rolodex card)

Printing Offset

Software Adobe Illustrator

Initial Print Run 1,000

Cost $5,000

Concept The puzzle conveys the idea of an illustrator who can work within the boundaries provided by an art director or designer and create work that will fit in with the concept at hand. This idea is underscored by the insert card, which bears the headline "Illustration That's Always Quite Fitting."

Special Visual Effect The shadowy illustrations in the puzzle mirror those the illustrator uses in his stationery (not shown here), tying this puzzle in with the rest of the illustrator's identity system.

Special Production Techniques The puzzle artwork was created with all type in place on an overlay; Rolodex cards (one with the illustrator's name and one with his agency's name) were ganged with the puzzle and colored with CMYK traps to avoid using another separation.

Cost-Saving Technique A "quickie printer" was used for the vertical insert cards.

Distribution of Piece The piece was hand-delivered and mailed to art directors, designers and art buyers at agencies and publishers; one bulk mailing was followed by smaller mailings on an as-needed basis.

Response to Promotion The response was very positive, with almost immediate response in several cases.

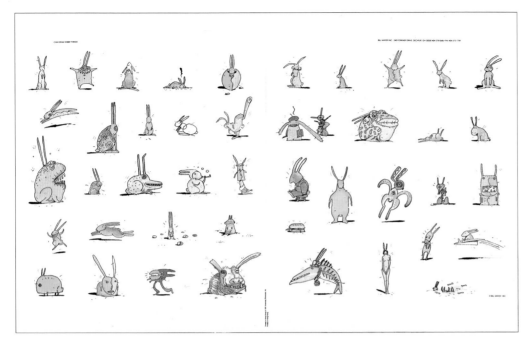

Art Directors/Studios Scott O'Leary/Southwestern Bell ("Can Draw Rabbit Things"); Alan Lidjii/Williamson Printing ("Bookworm"); David Lowey/VAR Business ("Computer Knight")

Designer/Studio Bill Mayer/Bill Mayer, Inc.

Illustrator Bill Mayer

Client/Service Bill Mayer, Inc./ illustration

Colors Four, process

Type Avant Garde

Printing Offset

Initial Print Run 50,000 ("Can Draw Rabbit Things"); 20,000 ("Bookworm" and "Computer Knight")

Concept An ongoing series of ads in illustrators' showcases, which have also been used as tear sheets distributed through direct mail, has continued to get the word out about Bill Mayer's illustration work. Each ad features Mayer's work for corporate or editorial clientele. "Can Draw Rabbit Things," for instance, was culled from a character development Mayer did for a Southwestern Bell advertisement; other pieces were originally commissioned by book and magazine art directors. The variety of artistic styles and subject matter from piece to piece effectively conveys Mayer's artistic versatility; Mayer's frequent use of a whole spread to showcase a single memorable image grabs more attention than a broad sampling of Mayer's work might have.

Seymour
roup
anne
roup

Client/Service Pushpin
Associates, New York, NY/illustra-
tors' representative
Paper Cross Pointe Genesis
Script Husk
Colors One, black
Type City Light (text), various
wood types (heads)
Printing Offset
Software QuarkXPress
Initial Print Run 6,000

Concept Inspired by sensational-
istic tabloids of the twenties and
thirties, this newsletter promotes
the services of Pushpin artists by
showing, not selling. In this piece,
Pushpin illustrators bring to life
mock-sensational news stories
about topics such as a musical version of *The Poseidon Adventure*, a
sighting of Elvis over an Istanbul
minimall, and a salesman named
Noel Shame who drove a housewife
to attempted murder. The only
clue to the self-promotional nature
of the piece is the response card
included within.
Cost-Saving Technique Printing
was donated by Berman Printing
Company, and paper was donated
by Cross Pointe, in exchange for
advertising within the piece.
Distribution of Piece The piece
was mailed once to previous and
potential clients.
Response to Promotion Most of
the response cards included in the
mailing were returned with positive feedback and queries for more
samples.

THE PUSHPIN EVENING SUN

A PUBLICATION FROM PUSHPIN ASSOCIATES   "E PLURIBUS TRIVIA"   VOLUME ONE /NUMBER ONE   FALL, 1992

MOIRA HAHN

SALESMAN DRIVES HOUSEWIFE BERSERK

**ATTEMPTED SALE,
ATTEMPTED MURDER!**

PLEASANTVILLE, OHIO "He wouldn't
leave me alone!" said Irene Rate, who
attempted to murder a pesky Acme "brush
man" late yesterday evening. Ms. Rate said
that the tenacious salesperson "just wouldn't
take no for an answer," as he continued to
pitch Acme's new *Miracle Brush* for over
six hours at the doorstep of Ms. Rate's tidy
suburban home.

Ms. Rate explained that she tried to turn
the salesman, Noel Shame, away politely,
but as he persisted, she became increas-
ingly more direct with him. "First I told him
that today wasn't a good day," she said.

"Then I told him I wasn't really interested.
I told him I had no money and I told him I
hated his products. Then I told him I hated
him *and* his products."

After four hours of hard sell, Rate says
she felt compelled to use more drastic mea-
sures to dissuade the salesman. "I asked
him into the kitchen and offered him a cool
drink of lye, but that only seemed to refresh
him. I was able to maneuver him into the
laundry room where I threw a noose made
of clothesline around his neck, but that
didn't stop him; it just made his voice sound
squeaky. In the height of fury, I whacked
him with an axe from the utility closet, but
it only hit him in the shoulder and he kept
coming at me saying, 'But ma'am, it's an

item no family can do without.'"

Finally, Ms. Rate ran to the rumpus
room and pulled out a .38 caliber long-
barrelled revolver that she kept hidden
under a fringed ottoman. Brandishing the
weapon at the salesman, she managed to
hold Shame at bay until they were dis-
covered by a delivery boy from the local
7-11 store, who called for help and then
recorded the mayhem with his trusty Kodak.

Mr. Shame told reporters from his hospital bed, "It is most important for a good
salesperson to be persistent. People need
my products whether they know it or not,
and I know that deep down inside she
wanted a *Miracle*."

Last year, Shame was hospitalized after

another no-sale in Poughkeepsie. "I thought
he was just about ready to order the whole
set, until he wheeled his baby grand piano
out a second-story window directly over
the front-door stoop where I was standing."

Ironically, Shame is not pressing charges
against Ms. Rate. "Salespeople," he says,
"have to be able to take rejection; it comes
with the territory. Besides, it's all relative
and she wasn't *that* bad."

When asked whether he plans to continue to pound the pavements after his
recovery, Shame said, "Of course. I love what
I do. I believe in the *Miracle;* selling the
line is lucrative and almost always exciting. I am a born salesman and I'll be a
'brush man 'til the day I die!"

WELL HELLO THERE.

WELCOME TO MY DIGITAL PORTFOLIO.

FEEL FREE TO BROWSE AT YOUR LEISURE.

CLICK TO CONTINUE

CLICK TO CONTINUE

CLICK TO CONTINUE

FOR MORE SAMPLES SEE:
1993 & 1994 WORKBOOK
1993 CREATIVE ILLUSTRATION
RSVP 19

Designer/Studio Scott Matthews/ Scott Matthews Illustration
Illustrator Scott Matthews
Client/Service Scott Matthews Illustration, St. Louis, MO/illustration
Type Lithos Bold (on screen), Dom Casual (label)
Software Macromind Director
Initial Print Run 200

Cost $1,000 (initial outlay; 50¢ each after)

Concept This computerized portfolio of Matthews' work, which takes no more than a few minutes to view, gives him a cost-efficient way to promote his illustration services. Since half of his work is digital, this format is also an efficient one for him: Its flexibility allows him to update his portfolio quickly and cheaply, and its uniqueness ensures it will be remembered.

Special Visual Effects After the initial greeting, the bulk of the portfolio consists of the presentation of an image, which then dissolves into the next image; this presentation is a surprising and playful way of engaging viewers' interest and enticing them to view the whole portfolio.

Distribution of Piece The piece was mailed sporadically to existing clients and select art directors.
Response to Promotion Response from recipients has been very positive; most commented that they had never seen illustration samples in this format, and they loved it; to date it has brought the illustrator $12,000 worth of work.

Art Director/Studio Arlen Schumer/Dynamic Duo
Designer/Studio Arlen Schumer/Dynamic Duo
Illustrators Arlen Schumer, Sherri Wolfgang
Silkscreen Printer Porcupine Graphics, Barnard, VT
Client/Service Dynamic Duo, Westport, CT/illustration
Colors Five, match
Type Hand-lettering
Printing Silkscreening
Initial Print Run 1,000
Cost $6,250

Concept This T-shirt promotion appeals to its art director audience by whimsically depicting a superhero art director pitted against headless, "sinister-suited" account executives—a concept as appealing to the recipient as it is an apt showcase for the Dynamic Duo's comic book illustration style. The figure of the art director wielding his T square like a weapon pays homage to Jack Kirby's Thor superhero, a fact acknowledged on the "spine" of the comic book. The only clue that the piece is promotional in nature appears on the back of the T-shirt, which credits the illustrators and gives their representative's phone number.

Distribution of Piece The piece was mailed at Christmas to representatives and past clients.

Response to Promotion The promotion brought the illustrators appreciation from the recipients, some calls for their portfolios, and many requests for more T-shirts.

ALAN LITHOGRAPH

Art Director/Studio James Cross/Cross Associates

Designers/Studios James Cross, Joseph Jacquez, Gary Trethaway, Vince Rini/Siegel & Gale/Cross Associates

Photographers Charles Imstepf (cover), Mercier-Wimberg Photography, various

Client/Service Alan Lithograph, Inglewood, CA/general commercial printing

Paper Potlatch Quintessence Gloss Cover (cover) and Gloss Text (photos); Simpson Starwhite Vicksburg Smooth Tiara (text) and Finish Text (calendar); Hopper Cardigan Tweed Text (flysheets)

Colors Four, process, plus one, match and spot varnish (text); four, process, plus two spot varnish and UV coating (cover)

Type Various

Printing Offset

Software Aldus FreeHand, Aldus TrapWise, Microsoft Word, QuarkXPress, Adobe Photoshop

Initial Print Run 5,250

Concept While this calendar featuring fine Los Angeles restaurants primarily promotes Alan Lithograph, it also serves as a great cross-promotion for the designers, photographers and restaurants involved in the piece. Fifteen restaurants get four pages each (one page is a recipe and three pages are photographs of the chefs and their restaurants); fifteen photographers, all of whom are credited in the front of the calendar, have taken the pictures. The rest of the piece consists of a week-by-week appointment calendar. The appointment calendar and recipes make this a promotion that will be useful to a broad cross section of its recipients; the design and pho-

tography make it a beautiful showcase of Alan Lithograph's expertise.

Special Visual Effects Hours of the day are indicated by clock icons on the calendar pages; in keeping with the food motif, the times meals traditionally take place are noted with plate and silverware icons.

Distribution of Piece The piece was mailed and hand-distributed to clients and prospective clients.

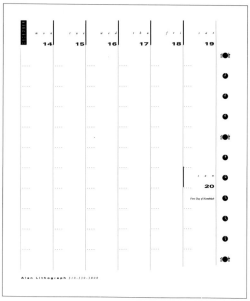

Art Director/Studio Craig Frazier/Frazier Design

Designer/Studio Craig Frazier/Frazier Design

Photographer Jock McDonald

Client/Service Jock McDonald, San Francisco, CA/photography

Paper Neenah Environment Desert Storm Wove (cover), Potlatch Vintage Velvet Cover (text)

Colors Six, black and match

Type Bodoni Antiqua, Bodoni Antiqua Italic

Printing Offset

Concept This simple booklet of toned black-and-white prints lets the pictures do the talking. The humorous photographs are printed, one image per spread, on glossy white paper; the facing page of each spread is a recycled stock on which the caption is printed. Using minimal text and the simplest of layouts focuses all of the viewer's attention on the photographs. The result is a simple yet expressive promotion that lets McDonald's work speak for itself.

Special Visual Effect Using a recycled stock in an earth tone for alternating pages lends each spread some warmth without competing with the photographs.

Distribution of Piece The piece was used as a leave-behind and was mailed to art directors, graphic designers and magazines.

PROMOTIONAL

PIECES FOR CLIENTS

Art Directors/Studio Todd Hart, Shawn Freeman/Focus 2

Designers/Studio Todd Hart, Shawn Freeman/Focus 2

Photographers Phil Hollenbeck, various

Illustrators Various

Client/Service Dallas Society of Visual Communications, Dallas, TX/creative association

Paper Various

Colors One to two, black and match

Type Various

Printing Offset

Software QuarkXPress, Aldus FreeHand, Adobe Photoshop

Initial Print Run 1,000

Cost None (materials and services donated)

Concept This dynamic newsletter provides members of the Dallas Society of Visual Communications with the latest information about happenings within the DSVC. The design, photography and writing— all by DSVC volunteers—are an inspiring demonstration of the talent to be found in the Dallas area; the content of the features is lively and engaging. The result is a newsletter that effectively promotes the DSVC by generating excitement about its activities.

Cost-Saving Techniques To cut costs and make production of the newsletter easier for the designers and printer, this version was a redesign of the original 15-by-21-inch version shown on pages 32 and 33; this version's limited number of colors, as well as its smaller 10½-by-15-inch format, helped achieve this goal.

Distribution of Piece The newsletter is mailed monthly to DSVC members.

Response to Promotion Membership and participation have continued to rise since the publication's institution.

ROUGH

Art Directors/Studio Todd Hart, Shawn Freeman/Focus 2

Designers/Studio Todd Hart, Shawn Freeman/Focus 2

Photographers Phil Hollenbeck, various

Illustrators Various

Client/Service Dallas Society of Visual Communications, Dallas, TX/creative association

Paper Various

Colors Four, process, and two, match

Type Various

Printing Offset

Software QuarkXPress, Aldus FreeHand, Adobe Photoshop

Initial Print Run 1,500

Concept This original version of the Dallas Society of Visual Communications newsletter (the current version is shown on page 31) uses a slightly different format to accomplish the same goal: to generate members' enthusiasm about DSVC activities.

Special Visual Effect Practically every issue features an article about a nationally known designer (usually one who has just spoken or who will soon speak at a DSVC meeting); the design of these features usually alludes to the designer's well-known style.

Distribution of Piece The publication is mailed monthly to DSVC members.

Response to Promotion It has resulted in a dramatic increase in membership and participation in DSVC events.

C.J. GRAPHICS, INC.

Art Director/Studio Ric Riordon/ The Riordon Design Group, Inc.
Designers/Studio Ric Riordon, Dan Wheaton/The Riordon Design Group, Inc.
Illustrator Dan Wheaton
Client/Service C.J. Graphics, Inc., Toronto, Ontario/printing and lithography
Paper Royal Impression Brilliant Gloss Text
Colors Four, process, and two, match
Type Heliotype, Mekanic, Futura Bold Condensed
Printing Offset
Software QuarkXPress, Adobe Photoshop, Adobe Illustrator
Initial Print Run 2,000
Cost $8,700

Concept This poster for a printer and lithographer employs a visual interpretation of the company's name to promote its services to the Toronto design community. This tongue-in-cheek approach also gives the company a chance to showcase its technical expertise with the creative use of varnish, metallics and process colors.
Special Visual Effects The sounding-out of the company's name was done in the four-square format of the company's logo; the *C* and *J* colored in the squares of the logo are depicted with a subtle varnish of gloss over the picture boxes.
Cost-Saving Technique The piece was designed in a trade-out for printing services.
Distribution of Piece The poster was originally given to clients at the company's Christmas party, but it is still being used as a leave-behind for new prospects.
Response to Promotion The piece has enhanced the company's profile in its community and has been greeted with positive feedback and requests for additional copies of the poster.

Art Director/Studio Carlos Segura/Segura Inc.

Designer/Studio Carlos Segura/ Segura Inc.

Photographers Masaaki Imamura, Shinichi Hiraki

Client/Service The Argus Press, Niles, IL/printing

Paper Brite White Esprit Laid (envelope), Reflections Gloss Cover (poster), Curtis Parchment Parchkin Riblaid (tissue)

Colors Two, match, and four, process

Type Isadora, Carta, Emigre 15, Bauer Bodoni

Printing Offset

Software QuarkXPress, Adobe Illustrator, Adobe Photoshop

Initial Print Run 3,000

Concept This six-color piece promoted Argus Press's seventieth anniversary, and its acquisition of a third six-color press, by offering recipients a six-color job printed at a four-color rate. But the best promotional pitch of all is the expert printing the piece demonstrates.

Special Visual Effects The semi-transparent paper—used to credit the design firm, the photographers and the writer—is covered throughout with watermarks that add extra texture and transparency to the paper. On the envelope, the words "a colorful celebration" are embossed and printed with clear eggshell foil, which makes the words appear opalescent. The borders of the poster itself are printed with a pale yellow ink pattern that gives the border the look of marbled paper.

Distribution of Piece This piece was hand-delivered on an as-needed basis to new leads.

LASERSCAN

Art Directors/Studio Russ Haan, Dino Paul/After Hours

Designer/Studio Dino Paul/After Hours

Photographers Jacques Barbey, Scott Baxter, Bob Carey, Juan Calvillo, Rick Gayle, John Gipe, Art Holeman, Tim Lanterman, Jeff Noble, Tim Pannel, Rodney Rascona

Illustrators Carolyn Fisher, Chuck Helt, Ann Hubbard, John Kleber, Steven King/Chromart, John Nelson

Client/Service Laserscan, Phoenix, AZ/color separating and electronic prepress services

Paper Potlatch Eloquence Gloss

Colors Four, process, and one, match, plus varnish

Type Bodoni Book, Gill Sans

Printing Offset

Software Adobe Illustrator, QuarkXPress, Adobe Photoshop

Initial Print Run 5,000

Concept This set of booklets promotes the services and expertise of a color separator by utilizing color at every opportunity. The covers use visual puns to draw viewers into the pieces ("Notes on Production" is illustrated with a photo of a crushed trumpet, for example); photographs and illustrations within the piece likewise reflect or interpret the verbal content of the spread in an unexpected way.

Special Visual Effect Layers of interlocking typography, with captions for the illustrations in red, maintain the energy level set by the vibrant photographs and illustrations.

Cost-Saving Technique Illustrators and photographers traded their services for color separations; a portion of the design firm's fee was also traded off.

Distribution of Piece The piece was distributed through sales representatives and was mailed as needed to new prospects and in response to inquiries.

Response to Promotion Laserscan gained some new clients and regained some former clients who had left because Laserscan did not then have electronic prepress capabilities.

Art Director/Studio Eric Rickabaugh/Rickabaugh Graphics

Designer/Studio Eric Rickabaugh/Rickabaugh Graphics

Photographer Paul Poplis

Illustrators Eric Rickabaugh, Michael Tennyson Smith, Fred Warter

Client/Service Byrum Lithographing, Columbus, OH/commercial printing

Paper Potlatch Quintessence Remaque Gloss Cover

Colors Ten, match, and four, process

Type Poster Bodoni, Spire (cover); Galliard Italic (text); Futura (caption); hand-lettering (heads)

Printing Offset

Software Aldus FreeHand

Initial Print Run 1,800

Cost $29,000

Concept Comparing the craftsmanship of Byrum's fine printing to the craftsmanship involved in creating a motion picture gave Rickabaugh Graphics an inviting way to showcase Byrum's printing abilities. The promotion consists of miniature posters, removable from the oversized booklet in which they're included, for four popular films. Vellum pages within the booklet—die-cut in a wide variety of creative ways—give the reader some background about the movie, so the poster itself can be uncluttered with text; the back of the poster ties the name of the movie to a printing process (e.g., *Ghostbusters* for ghosting, *The Shining* for metallic inks). This promotion is a beautiful and entertaining showcase of quality printing techniques.

Special Visual Effect The back of each page includes a color bar as a border, so there's no possibility of forgetting that this piece was designed to promote a printer.

Cost-Saving Technique Design and photography were traded for printing services.

Distribution of Piece The piece was mailed and hand-delivered on an as-needed basis to potential and current clients.

Response to Promotion The piece has successfully positioned Byrum Lithographing as a "premiere printer" and has opened doors to many new markets for the company.

GRAPHIC ARTS
CENTER

Art Director/Studio Kit Hinrichs/Pentagram Design
Designer/Studio Belle How/Pentagram Design
Photographers Terry Heffernan, Barry Robinson, Gary Braasch
Illustrators Gary Overacre, Will Nelson, Dan Picasso
Client/Service Graphic Arts Center, Portland, OR/printing
Paper Wyndstone Japanese (cover), Potlatch Eloquence Gloss Book (text), Simpson EverGreen (short page inserts)
Colors Four, match, and four, process
Type Futura Light, Bernhard Modern
Printing Offset, sheet-fed
Initial Print Run 15,000

Concept Since 85 percent of Graphic Arts Center's clients come from outside Oregon, and most spend at least one full day in the city, the format of an insider's guide to Portland was a fitting way to target this printer's clientele. And while the booklet is full of useful information about Portland, the need to promote GAC is not forgotten: Accompanying copy draws parallels between the city and GAC on virtually every spread. The result is a piece that sells the printer's services without looking like a printer's promotion.

Special Visual Effect On most pages, varnish is used only on the full-page photograph, not on the reversed-out blocks of copy, giving the photographs extra luster while making the copy easier to read.

Distribution of Piece The piece continues to be distributed by sales representatives, as well as through direct mail.

Response to Promotion GAC sales representatives continually get calls from clients asking for copies, and the piece has received many design awards, raising awareness for GAC among designers. The piece has generated new business for Pentagram as well.

Art Director/Studio Seymour Chwast/The Pushpin Group
Designer/Studio Greg Simpson/The Pushpin Group
Photographers Rick Muller (still lifes), Culver Pictures
Client/Service Ivy Hill Graphics, New York, NY/printing
Paper Potlatch Eloquence Gloss (text), Hammermill Antique White (cover, pop-ups)
Colors Four, process
Type Lightline Gothic (text), Egiziano (initials)
Printing Offset

Concept Two booklets—a series entitled "The P Chronicles"—were produced to promote Ivy Hill's printing services; the edition shown here is devoted to the art of package design. The first page of the booklet's interior consists of an introductory paragraph giving a brief history of packaging design; the next six pages are a visual survey of the same subject. The final page ties Ivy Hill's services in with the rest of the booklet's content.

Special Visual Effects Two of the packages in the center spread are three-dimensional; the Buckingham package pops up when the page is turned, and the package for crochet hooks can be opened to reveal realistic-looking metallic hooks.

Distribution of Piece Each booklet was mailed once to potential clients.

Response to Promotion Clients responded very positively, and the promotion has won several design awards.

Art Director/Studio John Sayles/ Sayles Graphic Design

Designer/Studio John Sayles/Sayles Graphic Design

Illustrator John Sayles

Client/Service University of California, Santa Barbara, CA/university

Paper Hopper Cardigan Text, chipboard

Colors Four, black and match

Type Hand-lettering; Futura Bold, Bodoni (text)

Printing Offset (interior), letterpress (cover)

Initial Print Run 5,000

Concept This brochure promotes the fraternity and sorority rush at the University of California at Santa Barbara. The theme, "Success by the Book," is carried out in the format of the piece's cover, which is shaped like a book; in the copy itself, which depicts Greek life as chapters from a book; and in the illustrations, which utilize book imagery. Layers of type, as well as the foldout format of the brochure text/poster, make the piece invitingly interactive.

Special Visual Effect The use of purple foil as an accent adds visual impact to the chipboard cover.

Special Production Techniques Hand-assembly of the mailing was done by an area agency for the handicapped. The top right portion of the foldout mailer was glued to the inside of the book "cover," so that the interior would be securely attached for mailing.

Distribution of Piece The piece was mailed once to incoming students.

CONTACT CREATIVE
SERVICES, INC.

Art Director/Studio Ric Riordon/
The Riordon Design Group, Inc.
Designers/Studio Ric Riordon,
Dan Wheaton/The Riordon Design
Group, Inc.
Photographer Stephen Grimes
Illustrator Dan Wheaton
Client/Service Contact Creative
Services, Inc., London, Ontario/
graphics and lithography
Paper Reflection Gloss (cover),
Gilbert Gilclear Medium Vellum
(flysheet), Reflection Gloss Text
(interior)
Colors Four, process with various
substitute inks, plus spot and
matte varnishes
Type Heliotype, Weiss, Industria,
Cochin
Printing Offset
Software Adobe Photoshop,
QuarkXPress, Ray Dream Designer,
Adobe Illustrator
Initial Print Run 5,000
Cost $35,000

Concept This booklet uses an
analogy between a theatrical performance and printing to promote
the services of a creative service
and lithographer. The stage facade
was built as a three-dimensional
model; this facade and the various
other elements were lit with fiber
optics and photographed. Compo-
sites of these photographs were
manipulated and overlaid with type
to result in the dreamlike illustrations; the theater motif is rein-
forced by the copy, which includes
appropriate quotations from
Shakespeare. The complexity of
these images gives Contact
Creative a chance to show off its
capabilities, as well as a way of
communicating to the viewer the
excitement of the printing process.
Special Visual Effect Using
process substitutes, as well as various matte and gloss varnishes
(some tinted), gives this booklet a
rich look.
Distribution of Piece The piece
has been mailed to and used as a
leave-behind for clients and potential clients.

THE PRINT COMPANY

Art Director/Studio Gunnar Swanson/Gunnar Swanson Design Office

Designer/Studio Gunnar Swanson/Gunnar Swanson Design Office

Client/Service The Print Company, Northridge, CA/offset and letterpress printing

Paper Gilbert Gilclear (outer wrap), Riegel PCW (interior)

Colors Two, black and match

Type Adobe Garamond

Printing Offset, letterpress

Software Adobe Illustrator

Initial Print Run 5,000

Concept The footprint motif of this booklet plays off the name of The Print Company, but the simplicity of the type treatment and the two-color format help the design reinforce the content of the copy, which emphasizes the old-fashioned nature of the business. The motif also reinforces the copy's message that the printer can lead inexperienced clients through the process step-by-step.

Cost-Saving Technique The whole piece was printed and die-cut by the client.

Distribution of Piece The piece was used primarily as a sales call leave-behind to potential printing customers.

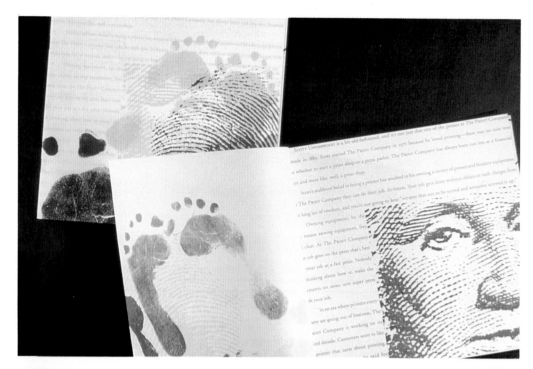

Art Director/Studio Alyn Shannon/Shannon Designs
Designer/Studio Alyn Shannon/Shannon Designs
Photographer Craig Perman
Client/Service Diversified Graphics Incorporated, Minneapolis, MN/full-service sheetfed printing
Paper Custom Color with Fibers Curtis Tweedweave (cover); Canson Satin, Prairie Flex (flysheets); Trophy Gloss Text (interior)
Colors Two, match, and four, process, plus varnish
Type Berkeley (text), Helvetica Compressed (headings)
Printing Offset
Software QuarkXPress, Aldus FreeHand
Initial Print Run 5,000
Cost $40,000

Concept Like the capabilities brochures of many printers, this piece showcases the abilities of the printer; unlike the others, this one also provides a warm introduction to the spirited team of craftspeople at DGI. The "Pulling Together" theme is carried out by the copy and by the numerous portraits of the people at DGI.

Special Visual Effect The elaborate printing of the vellum inserts, including spot four-color process and metallic ink, shows that DGI can produce even the trickiest print job.

Special Production Technique The booklet was bound with custom brass figures, which were then tied with string to create a "pulling together" effect.

Distribution of Piece It was mailed prior to an open house event, followed by ongoing mailings to designers, art directors, production coordinators and purchasing people.

Response to Promotion An overwhelming number of positive comments at the open house was followed by continuing positive feedback from recipients.

FRANK PARSONS PAPER COMPANY, INC.

Art Director/Studio Judy Kirpich/Grafik Communications, Ltd.

Designers/Studio Julie Sebastianelli, Lynn Umemoto/ Grafik Communications, Ltd.

Illustrator Henrik Drescher

Calligraphers Henrik Drescher, Melanie Bass

Client/Product Frank Parsons Paper Company, Inc., Landover, MD/paper

Paper Mead Signature Dull

Colors Four, process, plus one, match, and varnish

Type Bitstream Schneidler (paper names), Gill Sans (paper mills), Zapf Dingbats (paper codes)

Printing Offset

Software Aldus PageMaker

Initial Print Run 10,000

Concept The designers' original assignment was to redesign an ordinary paper cost comparison chart. The design team advised the client to restructure the chart to feature only the paper that Parsons carried. Then the team hired off-beat illustrator Henrik Drescher to give the charts maximum visual interest. The end result: a piece that's both useful and exciting, which recipients will keep and display.

Special Production Techniques Notecards, notepads, large and small charts for coded papers, and business reply envelopes were all printed on the same sheet of paper, with weights of paper changed during the print run.

Distribution of Piece The piece was mailed once to designers and printers; it was also distributed by paper sales representatives. Designers were rewarded for specifying Frank Parsons Paper by receiving a limited edition Henrik Drescher watch.

Response to Promotion The promotion has motivated designers and printers to spec Frank Parsons Paper, and has increased sales to Parsons.

Art Director/Studio Judy Kirpich/Grafik Communications, Ltd.
Designers/Studio Melanie Bass, Judy Kirpich/Grafik Communications, Ltd.
Photographers Pierre Goavec, Stephen John Phillips, Ira Wexler
Illustrators David Diaz, Henrik Drescher, Daniel Pelavin, Bob James, Evangelia Philippidis
Copywriter Jake Pollard
Client/Product Gilbert Paper, Menasha, WI/paper
Paper Gilbert ESSE Dark Gray Red Cover, Texture (cover); Gilbert ESSE Cover, Smooth, Light Gray Green and White Green (text)
Colors Three, match (text, glossary); various (illustrations)
Type Copperplate, Ribbon, hand-lettering
Printing Offset, with foil stamping, embossing and debossing
Software Aldus PageMaker

Concept This booklet demonstrates various printing, stamping and folding processes to show designers and printers how Gilbert ESSE paper performs. The theme of the booklet, "Questions Answered," is echoed by the motif of question marks and exclamation points used to illustrate these processes in the booklet.

Special Visual Effects The front of the booklet is die-cut so that the sunlike illustration on the first page is the bottom of the question mark on the front cover. The interior covers are riddled with hand-lettered question marks and exclamation points, as well as the words "questions," "answered" and "ESSE."

Special Production Techniques Images were grouped on a sheet to demonstrate a variety of techniques on each page. The same images and plates were used to show printing on both the textured and smooth finishes.

Distribution of Piece The piece was distributed through paper specification representatives and direct mail.

Design Director/Studio Steff Geissbuhler/Chermayeff & Geismar, Inc.

Designers/Studio Jim McKibben, Steff Geissbuhler/Chermayeff & Geismar, Inc.

Photographer Rodney Smith

Client/Service Crane & Co. business paper division, Dalton, MA/stationery paper manufacturer

Paper Crane's Crest R White (text), Crane's Parchment Fluorescent White (photographs)

Colors Gray plus four, match (text); two, black and one, gray (photos)

Type Univers 45 and 75

Printing Offset

Software QuarkXPress, Adobe Illustrator

Initial Print Run 8,000

Concept Couched within a cover of 100 percent cotton canvas, this 6½-by-6½-inch booklet provides an elegant view into the process of creating Crane's Crest R, a 100 percent cotton recycled paper. Black-and-white pictures provide a surprisingly beautiful depiction of Crane's papermaking process; the text describes the process with clarity and subtle lyricism. Both the content of the booklet and its thoughtful presentation emphasize Crane's painstaking attention to quality and details.

Special Visual Effects Every word in the half-cover's listing of parts of the papermaking process includes the letter *R*, all of which are lined up, printed in green ink, and engraved for maximum impact. Type treatments on each page visually correspond to the process they describe; the actual name of the stage is the only part of the booklet that appears in color. The watermark bearing the paper's name is intermittently visible on both the black-inked and the creme pages of the booklet.

Distribution of Piece The piece was distributed by mail and in response to requests from designers, merchants and specifiers.

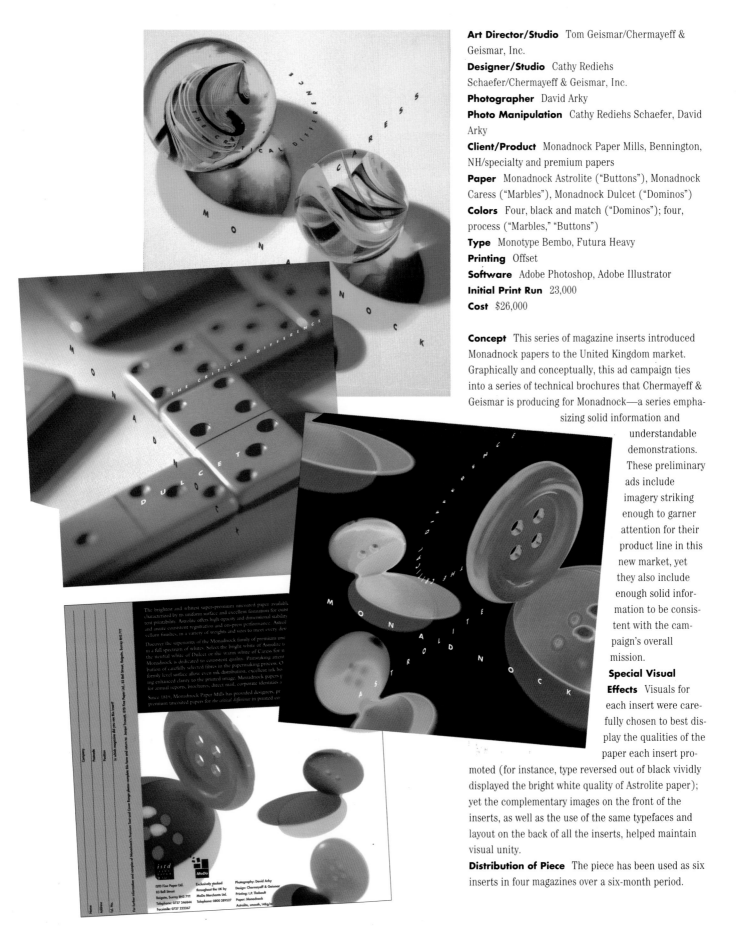

Art Director/Studio Tom Geismar/Chermayeff & Geismar, Inc.

Designer/Studio Cathy Rediehs Schaefer/Chermayeff & Geismar, Inc.

Photographer David Arky

Photo Manipulation Cathy Rediehs Schaefer, David Arky

Client/Product Monadnock Paper Mills, Bennington, NH/specialty and premium papers

Paper Monadnock Astrolite ("Buttons"), Monadnock Caress ("Marbles"), Monadnock Dulcet ("Dominos")

Colors Four, black and match ("Dominos"); four, process ("Marbles," "Buttons")

Type Monotype Bembo, Futura Heavy

Printing Offset

Software Adobe Photoshop, Adobe Illustrator

Initial Print Run 23,000

Cost $26,000

Concept This series of magazine inserts introduced Monadnock papers to the United Kingdom market. Graphically and conceptually, this ad campaign ties into a series of technical brochures that Chermayeff & Geismar is producing for Monadnock—a series emphasizing solid information and understandable demonstrations. These preliminary ads include imagery striking enough to garner attention for their product line in this new market, yet they also include enough solid information to be consistent with the campaign's overall mission.

Special Visual Effects Visuals for each insert were carefully chosen to best display the qualities of the paper each insert promoted (for instance, type reversed out of black vividly displayed the bright white quality of Astrolite paper); yet the complementary images on the front of the inserts, as well as the use of the same typefaces and layout on the back of all the inserts, helped maintain visual unity.

Distribution of Piece The piece has been used as six inserts in four magazines over a six-month period.

Art Director/Studio Kit
Hinrichs/Pentagram Design
Designer/Studio Belle
How/Pentagram Design
Photographers Geoff Kern, Barry
Robinson, Charly Franklin
Illustrators John Hersey, Greg
Spalenka, Wolf Spoerl, Phillipe
Weisbecker, Anthony Russo, Mark
Selfe, McRay Magleby, Takenobu
Igarashi
Client/Product Simpson Paper
Company, San Francisco, CA/paper
Paper Simpson Quest

Colors Twenty-four, match, and
four, process
Type City
Printing Offset
Initial Print Run 75,000

Concept This globally and environmentally themed campaign
introduced a line of recycled
papers. The name of the paper,
Quest, and the theme of the campaign, humanity's quest for solutions, ties in nicely with the fact
that this recycled paper takes

advantage of new technological
advances that do not harm the
environment. The recurring logo for
the campaign—a ball of scrap
paper resembling the globe—suggests the sophisticated and international character of the product. The
primary promotional booklet sup-
ports this motif by discussing global
change as a symptom of the quest
for solutions; by using an international team of designers, the look of
the booklet also reinforces this
theme. The result is a campaign as

sophisticated—both in design and
in content—as the paper it promotes.

Distribution of Piece Pieces are
in continual distribution—through
sales merchants and direct mail—
to designers, corporate clients and
printers.

Response to Promotion The promotion spurred great recognition in
the market, as well as continued
growth in sales.

Art Director/Studio Kit Hinrichs/Pentagram Design
Designer/Studio Belle How/ Pentagram Design
Illustrators Barbara Benthian, John Hersey, Will Nelson, Dave Stevenson
Client/Product Simpson Paper Company, San Francisco, CA/paper
Paper Simpson Quest Script
Colors Six, match, and four, process
Type City Light
Printing Offset, thermography
Initial Print Run 35,000

Concept Pentagram developed this portfolio of letterhead and business cards to introduce Quest Script, a paper designed especially for stationery usage, to the Quest line of recycled papers. Five preprinted stationery samples, each of which uses a different color of Script, are included in the folder, along with matching sample envelopes and business cards. The variety of samples demonstrates Script's ability to handle thermography, metallic inks, and a wide variety of ink coverages and color schemes. The folder also includes blank sheets and envelopes, so recipients can try out the paper.
Distribution of Piece The piece has been distributed through paper merchants and through direct mail to designers and print buyers.
Response to Promotion Sales have continued to grow since the introduction of the promotion.

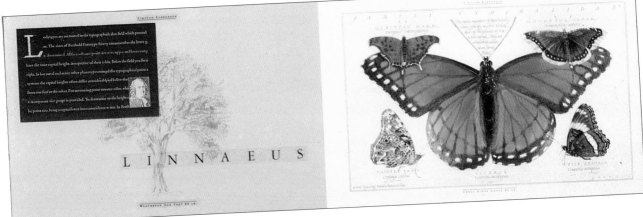

Art Director/Studio Kit Hinrichs/ Pentagram Design

Designer/Studio Belle How/ Pentagram Design

Assistant Designer/Studio Amy Chan/Pentagram Design

Photographers Bob Esparza, Kathryn Kleinman

Illustrators Dugald Stermer, Ward Schumaker, Dave Stevenson

Client/Product Simpson Paper Company, San Francisco, CA/paper

Paper Simpson EverGreen

Colors Four, match, and four, process

Type Copperplate Gothic Light, Garamond, Centaur, Englische Schreibschrift, Bodoni, Optical Character Recognition, Bernhard Modern, Bembo, Chevalier Caps Index, Cheltenham Old Style, Copperplate Gothic Heavy, Janson

Printing Offset

Initial Print Run 45,000

Concept This booklet introduces a collection of diverse yet related recycled papers by discussing a variety of famous natural collections, such as Noah's legendary menagerie and the Empress Josephine's collection of roses. Relating natural collections to this collection of recycled paper was a neat and logical fit; the wide variety of illustrations used to portray these legendary collections also gives viewers a chance to see the versatility of the paper over a wide range of ink coverages and illustration styles.

Distribution of Piece The piece has been distributed on a continuing basis through sales merchants and direct mail to designers, corporate clients and printers.

Response to Promotion The EverGreen line is now Simpson's most successful line of paper.

The story of Noah relates that, following divine guidance, he built a huge ark and collected animals and birds, two by two, to protect them from an apocalyptic rain of 40 days and 40 nights that flooded the face of the earth. This would make Noah the world's first animal preservationist and the first and, without a doubt, most successful person to launch an effort to save and encourage repopulation of endangered species. Over the millenia, Noah's menagerie has been depicted in nearly every medium, and Noah's Ark folkcraft and artwork have been avidly collected all around the world.

N O A H

SEVERAL CENTURIES AGO TO "LOOK UP YOUR CULPEPER" MEANT CONSULTING ACCEPTED HERBAL REMEDIES. APOTHECARIST NICHOLAS CULPEPER (1616-1654) APPLIED HIS KNOWLEDGE OF THE MEDICINAL USES OF COMMON PLANTS TO COMPILE THE FIRST ENGLISH HERBAL. PREVIOUSLY SUCH BOOKS WERE WRITTEN IN LATIN AND FEATURED EXOTIC REMEDIES THAT

ONLY THE WEALTHY COULD AFFORD. CULPEPER'S THE COMPLETE HERBAL, PUBLISHED IN 1649, HAS REAPPEARED IN 41 DIFFERENT EDITIONS OVER THE CENTURIES AND IS STILL IN PRINT. HIS ACCOUNT OF THE CURATIVE VALUE OF PLANTS THAT GROW AROUND US FOCUSED ATTENTION ON THE HEALING POWER OF NATURE, INSPIRING

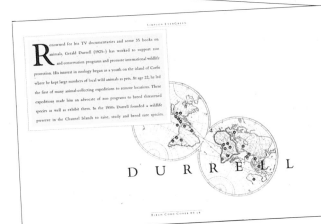

Renowned for his TV documentaries and some 35 books on animals, Gerald Durrell (1925-) has worked to support zoo and conservation programs and promote international wildlife protection. His interest in zoology began as a youth on the island of Corfu where he kept large numbers of local wild animals as pets. At age 22, he led the first of many animal-collecting expeditions to remote locations. These expeditions made him an advocate of zoo programs to breed threatened species as well as exhibit them. In the 1950s Durrell founded a wildlife preserve in the Channel Islands to raise, study and breed rare species.

D U R R E L L

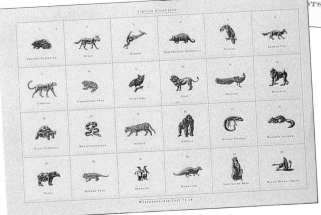

SIMPSON SUNDANCE LINGO

Art Director/Studio Kit Hinrichs/Pentagram Design

Designers/Studio Belle How, Amy Chan/Pentagram Design

Photographers Bob Esparza, Charly Franklin, Bybee Digital, Russell Kloer

Illustrators Dave Stevenson, Jack Unruh, Regan Dunnick, Lisa Miller, Erich Schreck, McRay Magleby, Will Nelson, Cathie Bleck, John Hersey, David Wilcox, Tim Lewis

Client/Product Simpson Paper Company, San Francisco, CA/paper

Paper Simpson Sundance

Colors Sixteen, match, and four, process

Type Cheltenham, Futura Extra Bold

Printing Offset

Software QuarkXPress

Initial Print Run 50,000

Concept This spiral-bound booklet uses a child's alphabet primer motif and a stepped-page format to introduce a new color palette for this existing line of recycled paper. The booklet begins by drawing an analogy between the character of Sundance Paper and the character of the New West; each subsequent page presents a letter of the alphabet and a word and definition of New West-themed Sundance "lingo" beginning with that letter. This motif is a fun and effective way to convey the revitalization of this existing line of papers.

Special Visual Effects The letters of the alphabet are interpreted in a variety of surprising and appropriate ways that tie into the word on the page (e.g., Old Faithful is depicted erupting from the middle of the letter *O*; the letter *G* appears in the shape of the Gila monster defined on the same page).

Distribution of Piece The piece has been distributed through paper merchants as well as through direct mail to designers, corporate buyers and printers.

Response to Promotion The promotion has been instrumental in revitalizing sales of this line of papers.

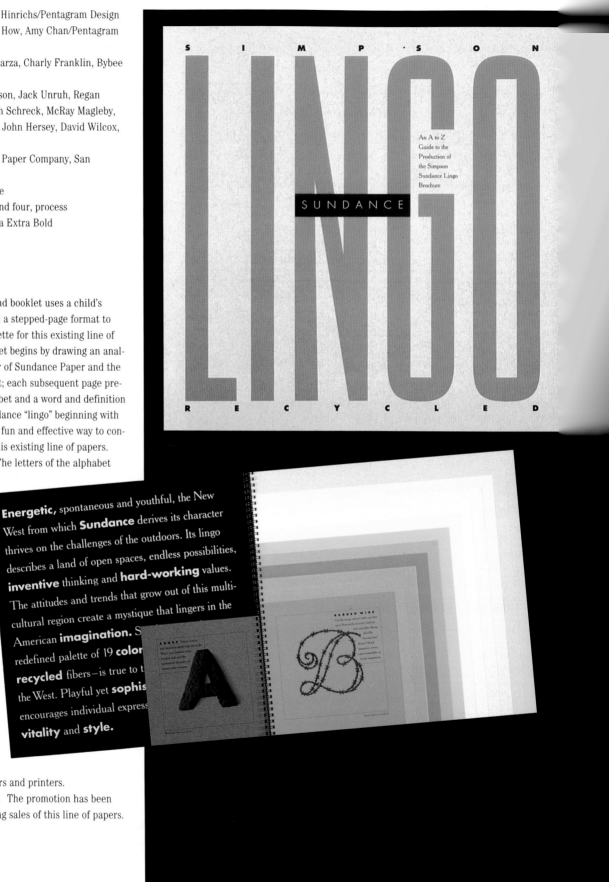

Energetic, spontaneous and youthful, the New West from which **Sundance** derives its character thrives on the challenges of the outdoors. Its lingo describes a land of open spaces, endless possibilities, **inventive** thinking and **hard-working** values. The attitudes and trends that grow out of this multicultural region create a mystique that lingers in the American **imagination.** S redefined palette of 19 **color** **recycled** fibers—is true to t the West. Playful yet **sophis** encourages individual express **vitality** and **style.**

Art Director/Studio Maureen Erbe/Maureen Erbe Design
Designers/Studio Maureen Erbe, Rita A. Sowins/Maureen Erbe Design
Photographers Various
Client/Service The Music Center of Los Angeles County, Los Angeles, CA/performing arts center
Paper Simpson EverGreen Birch

Text and Cover
Colors Four, black and match
Type Spire (divider headings), Cochin (text), Futura Book (opening text), Bureau Empire (section headings)
Printing Offset
Software QuarkXPress
Initial Print Run 13,500

Concept This booklet for the 1992-1993 Music Center Education Division promotes a roster of performing artists available for in-school performances and workshops. Vibrant shades of purple, teal and yellow-orange, with black as an accent, convey the excitement of the performers included in the book.

Special Visual Effect Layers of halftones, each printed in a different ink, give the divider pages the feel of a vibrant collage and further convey the feeling of excitement.
Distribution of Piece The piece was mailed once, followed by distribution throughout the year to schools, administrators and teachers.

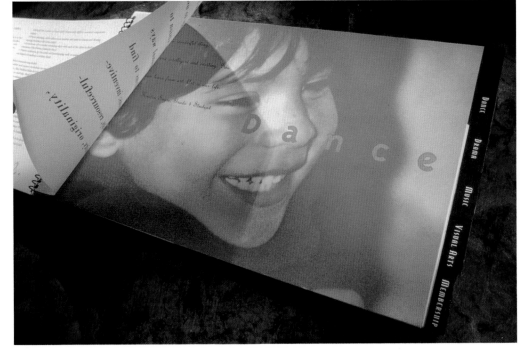

Art Director/Studio Maureen Erbe/Maureen Erbe Design

Designers/Studio Maureen Erbe, Rita A. Sowins/Maureen Erbe Design

Photographers Various

Client/Service The Music Center of Los Angeles County, Los Angeles, CA/performing arts center

Paper Simpson EverGreen White Cover and Text; vellum

Colors Four, black and match

Type Triplex Bold (text); Garamond 3 (subhead, quotations); Typo Upright (vellum sheets); Bodoni, Futura Demi (text subheads)

Printing Offset

Software QuarkXPress

Initial Print Run 13,500

Concept The theme of the 1993-1994 Education Division booklet is the abilities the arts foster in children's education. Highlighted are six abilities: skill, creativity, self-esteem, understanding, values and goals. At the beginning of each section, on a half sheet of vellum, one of the six abilities is defined; on the divider page following the vellum sheet, there appears a quotation from either an educator or a child about how the arts have enhanced their lives, along with an inviting photograph of a child's face.

Special Visual Effects The definitions on the vellum half sheets and the quotations on the following divider pages are positioned so that the two pieces of text intertwine when the two pages are together. Colors are used in the text only for heads and footers, with the body of text remaining black.

Cost-Saving Technique Halftones are printed with shades of bright, offbeat colors instead of the usual black, giving the piece a lively look for little additional cost.

Distribution of Piece The piece was mailed to schools, administrators and teachers, and distributed at their annual showcase event.

THE MUSIC CENTER OF LOS ANGELES COUNTY

Art Director/Studio Maureen Erbe/Maureen Erbe Design

Designers/Studio Maureen Erbe, Rita A. Sowins/Maureen Erbe Design

Photographers Henry Blackham (cover), Robert Millard, Frederic Ohringer, Dana Ross, Craig Schwartz, Martha Swope, Jay Thompson, Evan Wilcox

Photo Illustration Maureen Erbe Design

Client/Service The Music Center of Los Angeles County, Los Angeles, CA/performing arts center

Paper French Speckletone Madero Beach (text), Gilbert ESSE Texture Light Grey Red (cover)

Colors Four, match

Type Éurostile Bold (heads), Garamond 3 (text), Shelly and Copperplate 33 bc (quotations)

Printing Offset

Software QuarkXPress

Initial Print Run 11,500

Concept Coming on the heels of the 1992 riots in Los Angeles, this brochure was intended not only to raise funds but also to communicate how the arts can help to reunite the community through education and understanding. The palette of muted tones conveys the seriousness of the Center's mission; the treatment of the photographs conveys the feel of a work in progress, as well as a sense of urgency to the mission of the Music Center.

Special Visual Effect Right-hand pages are printed with a tint of green, with the headings and initial caps reversed out in white; this tint gives the booklet the feel of more than one type of paper.

Cost-Saving Technique No more than two inks are used on any given page, though four inks are used throughout the book; this gives the booklet the effect of many inks at a limited cost.

Distribution of Piece One mass mailing of five thousand copies was done to major donors and potential donors, with the rest distributed to potential donors throughout the year.

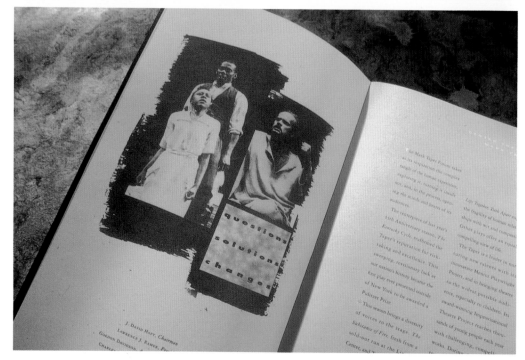

Art Director/Studio Clifford Stoltze/Stoltze Design

Designers/Studio Kyong Choe, Clifford Stoltze, Peter Farrell, Rebecca Fagan/Stoltze Design

Photographers Various

Illustrators Various

Client/Service Massachusetts College of Art, Boston, MA/art education

Paper Redap Matte, Island Resolve Bond, Champion Benefit

Colors Two, match, and four, process (cover); three, match (interior)

Type Meta, New Baskerville, Trixie

Printing Offset

Software QuarkXPress, Aldus FreeHand

Initial Print Run 30,000 (15,000 with this cover)

Cost $79,860

Concept This Massachusetts College of Art catalog called for a playful, experimental approach; unconventional uses of typography, layouts and color help give this book a look that will appeal to the type of student MCA wants to attract: a student with cutting-edge artistic sensibility.

Special Visual Effects The unusual use of fluorescent and metallic inks throughout the book gives it an up-to-the-minute look; using these inks for the halftones as well helps liven up some potentially prosaic photographs.

Cost-Saving Technique Photographs and illustrations were donated by students and faculty.

Distribution of Piece The piece was mailed continually to potential students.

Response to Promotion This catalog helped MCA increase enrollment.

EMPSON, INC.

Designers/Studio Susan English, Gregg Glaviano, Judy Kirpich/ Grafik Communications, Ltd.

Illustrator Michael Crampton

Client/Service Empson (USA), Inc., Alexandria, VA/wine importer and wholesaler

Paper Hopper Cardigan Eggplant (tourbook cover); Fox River Confetti Kaleidoscope, Hopper Cardigan White (tourbook interior); Potlatch Vintage Velvet Cover (menus)

Colors Three, match and black

Type Berkeley, Weiss

Printing Silkscreening (invitation shells, tourbook covers, press kit folders), offset (interior)

Software Aldus PageMaker, Adobe Illustrator

Initial Print Run 5,000 (invitation shells); 1,000 (tourbooks); 5,000 (wine menu shells); 1,000 (press kit folders)

Cost $40,000

Concept This promotion was designed to build an image for Empson USA and its Tuscan wines, as well as to introduce four Tuscan growers and their wines through a four-city tasting tour. Instead of relying on a single logo for the whole campaign, three illustrations were developed, each conveying an aspect of producing or enjoying wine. A palette of ink colors and paper stocks further broadened the look, so it could be applied in a variety of ways. The result is a promotion with a fresh, lively, yet sophisticated look.

Special Visual Effects The judicious use of metallic inks, both for the wine menu shells and as an accent in the tourbook text, gives this promotion the necessary deluxe feel. Depicting the wine labels on the interior of the wine menu shells is an unusual and visually appealing touch.

Special Production Technique Silkscreening turned out to be slightly less expensive than offset, and allowed use of truly opaque colors on dark stock.

Cost-Saving Technique Overrun on the tourbook covers, ganged with the invitations, will allow new books to be produced for subsequent tours less expensively.

Distribution of Piece The invitations were mailed; the rest of the pieces were primarily distributed at wine-tasting events.

Response to Promotion The promotion gave the client a savvy, professional and experienced image.

Art Director/Studio Carlos Segura/Segura Inc.
Designer/Studio Carlos Segura/Segura Inc.
Photographer Geof Kern
Client/Service John Cleland, Chicago, IL/writer
Paper Mohawk UltraFelt
Colors Two, black and match
Type Centaur (body), old typewriter (cover)

Printing Offset
Software QuarkXPress, Adobe Photoshop
Initial Print Run 3,000

Concept This promotion for a technical writer plays off the cliché, "A picture is worth a thousand words." This piece conveys the importance of those maligned "thousand words" with the most appropriate medium: the writer's own words. This cerebral approach is made more accessible by its five-by-seven-inch booklet format, surreal illustrations, and a varied and exciting typographical treatment.
Special Visual Effects While the booklet at first glance appears to be printed with black ink only, a closer look shows that it is printed with a combination of black and dark brown ink; this dark brown ink gives the photo-illustrations the feel of fine art. An article from the *Wall Street Journal* cited by the writer folds out of the booklet; the paper on which the article is printed effectively mimics newsprint.
Distribution of Piece The piece was mailed on a continuing basis to chief executive officers.

MAJOR LEAGUE
BASEBALL PROPERTIES

Designers/Studio Kathryn Klein, James Skiles, Tim McGrath, Gorham Palmer/Midnight Oil Studios

Photographer John Van S

Illustrators James Skiles, Kathryn Klein, Tim McGrath

Client/Service Major League Baseball Properties, New York, NY/licensing of baseball team identities

Paper Champion Hopsack (cover), Warren L.O.E. Dull Coated (interior)

Colors Four, process, and two, match

Type Various

Printing Offset with engraving

Initial Print Run 5,000

Cost $75,000

Concept The nostalgic feel of this campaign is an appropriate way to appeal to potential licensees and corporate sponsors of major league baseball. While the brochure includes plenty of financial and demographic statistics designed to persuade recipients that baseball is a worthy investment, the visual presentation follows through on the soft-sell look of the rest of this campaign. Additional collateral—the baseball cap, baseball, and uniform shirt—makes the nostalgic feel of the campaign even more tangible for recipients.

Special Visual Effect In the capabilities brochure, photographs of crowds at baseball games are screened out and used as background patterns on some spreads—a subtle way of underscoring the popularity of baseball.

Distribution of Piece The pieces were hand-delivered and mailed over a three-year period to potential licensees and sponsors.

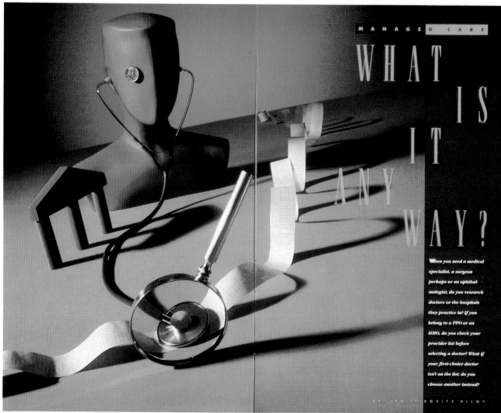

Art Director/Studio Eric Rickabaugh/Rickabaugh Graphics
Designer/Studio Eric Rickabaugh/Rickabaugh Graphics
Editor Steven M. Shivinsky, APR
Photographers Chas Krider, Larry Hamill, Ron Rovtar
Illustrators Michael Linley, C.S. O'Leary, Larry Hamill, Al Hirschfeld
Client/Product Grant Medical Center, Columbus, OH/hospital newsletter
Paper Mead Signature Gloss
Colors Two, match, and four, process
Type Futura, Garamond
Printing Offset
Software Adobe Photoshop, Aldus FreeHand, Aldus PageMaker
Initial Print Run 7,000
Cost $20,000

Concept This biannual newsletter needs to promote a hospital to a diverse audience that includes hospital donors, employees, board members and the general public. The only thing all the recipients have in common is a lack of time, so the publication needs to be visually exciting to entice recipients into reading it.

Special Visual Effect Dynamic and varied type treatments give vitality to the traditional typefaces used for the bulk of the publication.

Cost-Saving Technique Producing the publication on desktop technology saved many dollars in typesetting.

Distribution of Piece The piece is mailed twice yearly to hospital employees, board members and donors, as well as the general public.

Response to Promotion The publication has become highly anticipated and has helped to establish a positive image for Grant Medical Center.

Art Directors/Studios Jackson and Eric Boelts/Boelts Bros. Design; Laura Perry/Aldus Corporation
Designers/Studio Jackson and Eric Boelts/Boelts Bros. Design
Illustrators Jackson and Eric Boelts
Client/Product Aldus

Corporation, Seattle, WA/software
Colors Four, process
Printing Offset
Software Aldus FreeHand
Initial Print Run 25,000
Cost $10,000

Concept When creating the packaging for Aldus FreeHand, the

designers' challenge was to find a solution that both conveyed the freedom of the program and demonstrated its capabilities. Working in FreeHand, they created this dynamic illustration of a frolicking figure who has left the cares of the city behind him. Since the program is most likely to be used by designers

at work (quite possibly in a big city), this illustration on the software packaging cleverly suggests that, by giving you the artistic freedom you've always wanted, FreeHand will make you feel as if you're not working.

Art Director/Studio Jack Anderson/Hornall Anderson Design Works

Designers/Studio Jack Anderson, Julie Tanagi-Lock, Mary Hermes, David Bates, Julie Keenan/Hornall Anderson Design Works

Illustrator Julia LaPine

Client/Service Starbucks Coffee Company, Seattle, WA/coffee importer, roaster and retailer

Paper Kraft (shopping, lunch and pastry bags); corrugated kraft (gift box); coated matte (syrup labels); clay-coated (coffee bags)

Colors Four, process, with other colors substituted for CMYK (shopping bags); three to six, black and match (additional packaging)

Type Univers Condensed, hand-lettering

Printing Flexography

Software Aldus FreeHand

Concept This complete redesign of packaging for the rapidly growing coffee company reflects Starbucks' commitment to high quality, both in product and personnel. Warm colors and intimate, sophisticated illustrations reflect the company's personality; details like gold leaf foil stamping on the labels and fully illustrated gift boxes and tissue paper reflect the company's attention to detail in all aspects of its operation. The prominent illustration of a coffee roaster suggests the company's respect for the art of coffee roasting. The recurring steam patterns represent the freshness of Starbucks' products.

Special Production Technique Using recycled kraft paper and water-based inks is in line with Starbucks' commitment to the environment.

Response to Promotion Consumer reaction to the packaging has been extremely positive, and Starbucks' reputation for quality has continued to grow rapidly since the release of the packaging.

CALIFORNIA
Y

Julia Chong

lia Chong

Tam Design

Illustrator Mercedes McDonald

Client/Product Southern
California Gas Company/natural
gas

Paper Warren Lustro Recycled
Gloss

Colors Four, process, and one,
black plus two varnishes

Type Garamond Condensed,
Univers

Printing Offset

Software Microsoft Word,
QuarkXPress, Adobe Illustrator

Initial Print Run 25,000

Concept This brochure, which
was developed to promote the
usage of gas appliances in model
homes, fulfills its mission in a
warm, inviting way.

Special Visual Effects Color
bands on the top of each leaflet
were chosen to complement the
illustration on that page; the small
triangle of white at the top of each
leaflet gives the page a notched
effect and mirrors the shape of the
folder itself.

Cost-Saving Technique Designing the booklet so that each product is promoted on a separate
leaflet ensures that, if one of the
leaflets needs to be changed, the
whole booklet will not have to be
reprinted.

Distribution of Piece The piece
was distributed at model homes to
prospective home buyers, to
encourage the use of gas appliances.

Response to Promotion Customers responded very positively to the
piece, and it has been reprinted a
number of times. It has also resulted in increased home sales and gas
appliance sales.

PAM THUM

Art Director/Studio Ric Riordon/ The Riordon Design Group, Inc.
Designers/Studio Ric Riordon, Dan Wheaton, Shirley Riordon/The Riordon Design Group, Inc.
Photographer Ron Keith
Client/Service Benson Music Group, Inc., Nashville, TN/music recording and publishing
Paper Beckett Concept, Sandstone Text
Colors Four, process, and one, match
Type Lithos, Futura Condensed
Printing Offset
Software QuarkXPress, Adobe Photoshop, Adobe Illustrator
Initial Print Run 3,000
Cost $9,500

Concept This prerelease promotional CD utilizes a booklet format to make it stand out from the usual jewel boxes that program directors and music press receive. The back of the folder is vertically die-cut to hold the CD; a minibooklet with information about the recording artist is stapled in the front of the folder, and the whole piece is held together by a Velcro fastener. The final effect is a warm and tactile promotion.

Special Visual Effects The shape of the die-cut front cover is echoed in the shape of the background screen tints on each spread, which employ lighter tints of the blue and olive used for the cover.

Cost-Saving Technique Using the same grid for each spread helped save on design time. Application of metallic ink only on the inside cover added a deluxe look at minimal cost; uncoated stock made varnishes unnecessary.

Distribution of Piece The piece was mailed and hand-delivered to gospel radio program directors and disc jockeys, music press and bookstores.

Response to Promotion The promotion helped Pam Thum get noticed in a competitive marketplace.

WORCESTER COMMON FASHION OUTLETS

Designers/Studio Kathryn Klein, James Skiles, Tim McGrath, Gorham Palmer/Midnight Oil Studios

Photographers Picture Perfect USA, Stock Boston, Bobby DiMarzo

Illustrators Kathryn Klein, Paul Gauguin (courtesy of Worcester Art Museum)

Client/Service New England Development/mall development

Paper Warren L.O.E. Dull Creme

Colors One, match, and four, process

Type Avenir, Matrix

Printing Offset

Software Adobe Illustrator

Initial Print Run 2,500

Cost $50,000

Concept This booklet uses a vibrant color palette, foldout pages, and lots of illustrations to convey the excitement of a new factory outlet development. To convince potential tenants that the Worcester area is ideal for an outlet mall, the booklet includes plenty of supporting geographical and demographic information about the area—but the wealth of maps and charts, as well as their beautiful presentation, makes this information accessible and engaging.

Special Visual Effect The cover and a portion of the interior are varnished with a version of one of the maps printed elsewhere in the booklet.

Distribution of Piece The piece was distributed at trade shows and mailed to potential retail tenants of the development.

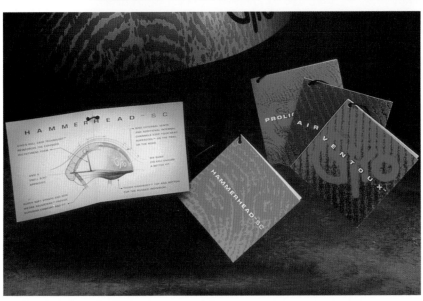

Art Director/Studio Jack Anderson/Hornall Anderson Design Works

Designers/Studio Jack Anderson, David Bates, Lian Ng/Hornall Anderson Design Works

Client/Product Giro Sport Design, Soquel, CA/bicycle helmets and accessories

Paper Laminated E-flute cardboard (packaging)

Colors Three, match

Type Microstyle

Printing Offset

Software Aldus FreeHand, Adobe Photoshop

Concept This redesign of Giro's helmets and subsidiary packaging blends the messages of fashion and technology, and conveys an image of high-quality merchandise. The designers' challenge was to incorporate the existing logo into a redesign that would be cohesive over a line of products, yet would distinguish individual projects from one another. Cohesion was maintained by keeping the logo placement and the rest of the helmet and packaging layout consistent; distinction was created by varying the colors used for each product and its packaging—with the colors targeted to appeal to the different audiences at which each product was aimed.

Special Visual Effect The striated, fingerprintlike pattern throughout the design gives both the helmets and their packaging a distinctive look.

Response to Promotion The packaging helped create a strong brand presence for Giro in the retail marketplace.

Art Director/Studio Kathryn Klein/State of the Art

Designer/Studio James Skiles/ Midnight Oil Studios

Photographers Jonathan Klein, John Van S

Illustrator Kathryn Klein

Client/Service Massachusetts Port Authority, Boston, MA/transportation

Paper Beckett Cambric (folder, letterhead), Warren L.O.E. Dull (brochure)

Colors Five, match (letterhead); four, process, plus one, match (brochure); one, match (folder)

Type Copperplate Gothic, Bernhard Modern, Ribbon, Skyline

Printing Offset

Software Adobe Illustrator

Initial Print Run 5,000

Cost $15,000

Concept This campaign promotes the convenience of using CruisePort Boston's facilities as a point of departure or stopping point for pleasure cruises. Brochure copy emphasizes the convenience of the Black Falcon Cruise Terminal's Boston location, as well as the facility's operational excellence. The primarily blue color scheme and the use of flag and anchor symbols give the campaign an appropriately nautical flavor, while the elegant use of type and illustrations gives the piece an upscale feel that suits the Boston location.

Special Visual Effects The back of the brochure folder where representatives' business cards are inserted is die-cut in a wave pattern. Both the blue border on the front of the brochure and the blue back cover are subtly printed in a darker match blue with small illustrations of lobsters, sea gulls, and other animals associated with harbor areas.

Distribution of Piece Pieces were distributed to cruise line directors through direct mail and through trade shows.

Response to Promotion The campaign helped to increase CruisePort Boston's business.

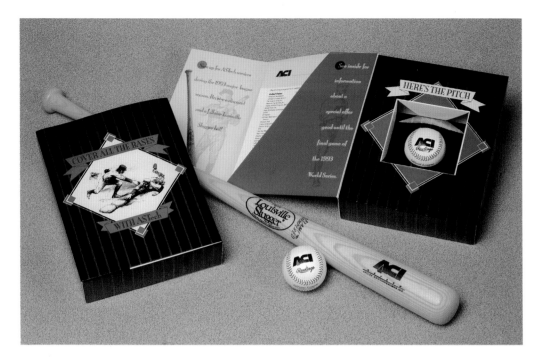

Art Director/Studio Dave Webster/Webster Design Associates, Inc.

Designer/Studio Dave Webster/Webster Design Associates, Inc.

Illustrator Dave Webster

Client/Service Applied Communications, Inc., Omaha, NE/tandem computer system consultation

Colors Four, match, and four, process

Type Burlington (cover), Garamond (text)

Printing Offset

Software Aldus FreeHand

Initial Print Run 500

Cost $15,000

Concept This four-phase campaign for a computer consultation firm is themed "Cover all the bases"; the promotion uses this baseball theme to suggest that even the best computer system managers need the "pinch-hitting" services of a consulting firm such as ACI's ASTech division. The first phase (upper left) consisted of a box with an ACI-emblazoned baseball inside. The second phase (lower left) was a self-mailer that featured a set of mock baseball cards that pop up when the self-mailer is opened; the cards, which are fully detachable, feature MVPs on the ASTech team, as well as their "stats." An ACI baseball cap and baseball bat rounded out the campaign. The promotion followed the baseball season and effectively targeted its primarily male demographic; this promotion's cleverness and consistency—both in look and theme—worked for the client.

Distribution of Piece The pieces were mailed to a list of computer system managers.

Response to Promotion The promotion generated an 87 percent awareness rate and a 17 percent response rate in its audience; to date, $1.2 million in revenue can be traced to this campaign.

CASA DE SAN PEDRO

Art Directors/Studio Russ Haan, Todd Fedell/After Hours
Designer/Studio Todd Fedell/After Hours
Illustrator Robert Case
Client/Service Casa De San Pedro, Sierra Vista, AZ/environmentally sensitive bed and breakfast
Paper Handmade from bed-and-breakfast site materials by Catherine's Rare Papers (cover)
Colors Two, match
Type Journal
Printing Offset
Software QuarkXPress, Adobe Illustrator
Initial Print Run 200
Cost $4,000

Concept This brochure, along with the project's financial prospectus, was sent to potential investors of an environmentally sensitive bed and breakfast. The brochure's purpose was to communicate what the prospectus alone could not convey: the spirit of the project. The lyrical copy is a fictional account of one visitor's experience there and is accompanied by illustrations that have the feel of woodcuts. The paper is handmade from site earth and fibers, and the brochure is held closed with a piece of brush from the site; the booklet is hand-stitched, and the inks are soy-based. All these details add up to a piece that's uniquely appropriate for its message.

Special Visual Effect The front cover is embossed with a bird logo, in keeping with the environmental theme.

Distribution of Piece The piece was mailed to potential investors of the project.

Response to Promotion The bed and breakfast was sufficiently funded.

Designer
David Col
Communi

Writers
Soter

Illustrato

Client/Service National Air and Space Museum, Washington, D.C./museum

Paper Potlatch Eloquence Cover

Colors Three, match

Type Bodoni

Printing Offset

Software Aldus PageMaker, QuarkXPress

Initial Print Run 500

Cost $14,000

Concept The primary objective of this booklet was to raise funds for a new gallery called "How Things Fly," at the National Air and Space Museum. The booklet illustrated the need for an interactive, hands-on flight exhibit by being an interactive piece, complete with questions and fold-out answers on the principles of flight. The early questions in the booklet are flight-related, but later questions such as "How can I help get the gallery off the ground?" help further the fund-raising goals of the booklet. The accessible tone—its bright color palette, its six-by-six-inch format, and its humorous copy and illustrations—make this booklet far more inviting than the average fund-raising brochure.

Special Visual Effect Left-hand pages and foldout interiors use details from blueprints, sketches and drawings from the "How Things Fly" collection.

Cost-Saving Technique The job was printed three over three plus varnish with one ink change, but because it was plasticoil-bound, it looks like a four-color job.

Distribution of Piece The piece was first handed out by NASM's Office of Development at the 1993 Paris Air Show; this was followed with small mailings to corporate executives and chief financial officers.

Art Director/Studio Maureen Erbe/Maureen Erbe Design

Designers/Studio Maureen Erbe, Rita A. Sowins/Maureen Erbe Design

Photographer Henry Blackham

Author Aileen Farnan Antonier

Client/Service Chronicle Books, San Francisco, CA/book publishing

Paper Glossy Japanese House Stock

Colors Four, process

Type Futura Bold (text); Ribbon, Bureau Empire, Hobo, Raleigh Gothic (headlines)

Printing Offset

Software QuarkXPress

Initial Print Run 15,000

Concept This book, entitled *Made in Japan*, features a collection of Japanese transistor radios from the fifties and sixties. The text and visuals point out how the Japanese appropriated American design and popular culture to sell their radios to the American market, and in turn invented a unique art form. The colors, graphics and typography in the book are all based on design devices from the radios themselves.

Special Visual Effect Typographic and graphic elements were chosen to complement both the radios and the copy presented on each spread; for instance, the spread on "googie" architecture is replete with the futuristic boomerangs and delta shapes that architecture was known for, and the spread on op art features a black-and-white checked background.

Distribution of Piece The piece was sold through bookstores and gift shops.

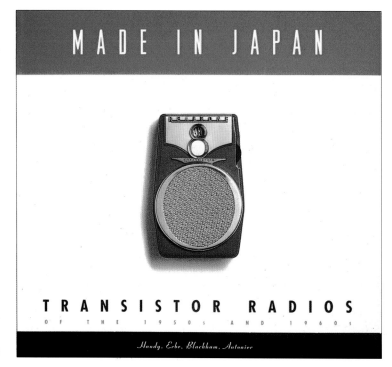

INVITATIONS AND
EVENT PROMOTIONS

Designers/Studio Melanie Bass, Julie Sebastianelli, Richard Hamilton, Jim Jackson, Jake Pollard, Andres Tremols, Pam Johnson/Grafik Communications, Ltd.

Illustrators Julie Sebastianelli, Melanie Bass

Copywriter Jake Pollard

Client/Event The American Institute of Graphic Arts, Washington, D.C./annual film night

Paper Champion Carnival White Text and Cover

Colors Three, black and match

Type Futura, Univers, Berkeley, Lubalin Graph

Printing Offset

Software Aldus FreeHand

Initial Print Run 2,500

Cost None (materials and services donated)

Concept This unique flip-book invitation for the AIGA's annual film night held to the spirit of the animated films to be shown: By using enigmatic images and letter-forms in motion, as did many of the films in the program, the invitation appeals to the same people who would enjoy the event itself.

Special Visual Effects The flip book begins with a mysterious black shape that slowly begins to rise and is surrounded by the floating letters

A, I, G and A; these letters flip into place on the black shape as a face, and then the lines that form the hair on the head fly upward and transform into a cord on a screen—which lowers to reveal the name of the program.

Special Production Techniques Since there was no budget for perfect binding, the booklet was top-stitched, and the staples were hidden by a longer sheet that wrapped around and folded over the back cover. The booklet was printed on one form, and the number of images was determined by how many could be printed on one sheet.

Cost-Saving Technique Materials and services for the invitation, and the rest of the function, were donated: among others, Champion International donated the paper; Huffman Press donated the enve-lope printing; Specialties Bindery, Inc. donated the binding, Peake Printers the printing, and OMEGA the output.

Distribution of Piece The piece was mailed once, two weeks before the event, to AIGA members, local designers, photographers, illustra-tors and filmmakers.

Response to Promotion The event sold out.

VAUGHN WEDEEN CREATIVE

Art Directors/Studio Rick Vaughn, Steve Wedeen/Vaughn Wedeen Creative

Designer/Studio Rick Vaughn/Vaughn Wedeen Creative

Illustrator Rick Vaughn

Production Artist Stan McCoy

Client/Event Vaughn Wedeen Creative, Albuquerque, NM/tenth anniversary party

Paper Rock-Tenn pasted chipboard (pages); Neenah UV/Ultra II (band)

Colors Two, match (pages); one, match (band)

Type Linoscript, Franklin Gothic Heavy

Printing Silkscreening (pages), laser printing (band)

Software QuarkXPress

Initial Print Run 400

Concept This graphic design studio decided to hold an open house party to commemorate its tenth anniversary and to show off its newly redecorated and expanded studio space. This chipboard booklet invitation plays off the idea of "tens" with a series of illustrations relating to the concept—a ten-gallon hat, the Ten Commandments—and then, on the last page, uses copy full of "ten"-related puns to issue the actual invitation.

Special Visual Effects The booklet is bound with a silver-tipped bolo tie, in keeping with the design firm's Southwestern locale. The actual "ten" object in each illustration is printed in red ink; the rest of the illustration is in blue.

Cost-Saving Techniques Using two colors on an inexpensive stock and hand-binding the booklet helped keep costs down.

Distribution of Piece The piece was hand-delivered or mailed to clients, vendors, family and friends of Vaughn Wedeen.

Response to Promotion The turnout to the party was great, and people said the evening was a perfect "ten."

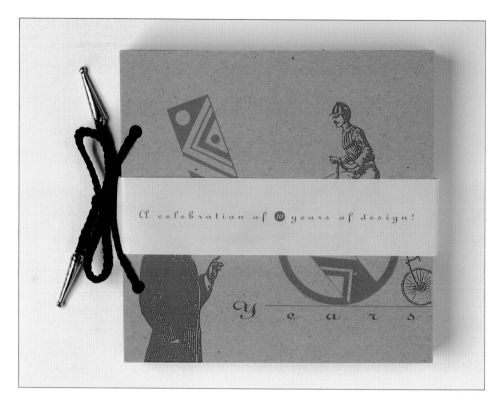

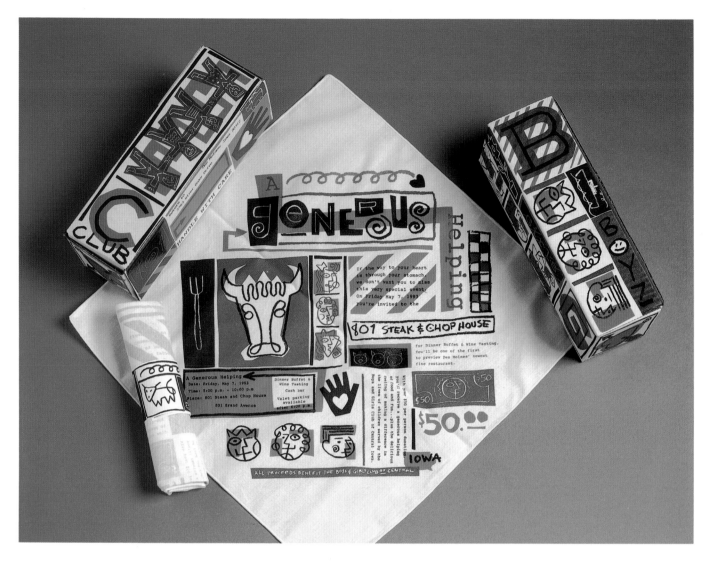

Art Director/Studio John Sayles/ Sayles Graphic Design

Designer/Studio John Sayles/ Sayles Graphic Design

Illustrator John Sayles

Client/Event Boys and Girls Club of Central Iowa, Des Moines, IA/benefit dinner

Paper Corrugated cardboard (mailer), Hopper White (return card)

Colors Four, match

Type Hand-lettering, typewritten

Printing Screenprinting (mailer, napkin); offset (return card)

Initial Print Run 250

Concept This invitation to a benefit dinner at a local steak restaurant comes in a fitting format: a napkin. The childlike illustrations reflect the beneficiary of the din-

ner, the nonprofit Boys and Girls Club of Central Iowa. The vibrantly screenprinted box that houses the napkin ensures this invitation won't be lost in a stack of mail.

Special Visual Effect The invitation is rolled up like a napkin with a paper "napkin ring" that bears the name of the Boys and Girls Club.

Cost-Saving Techniques Because of the low print run, screenprinting

the mailer saved money in production. Paper and printing were donated by local printers.

Distribution of Piece The piece was mailed once to Des Moines residents.

Response to Promotion Over four hundred people attended, raising more than $20,000 for the Boys & Girls Club.

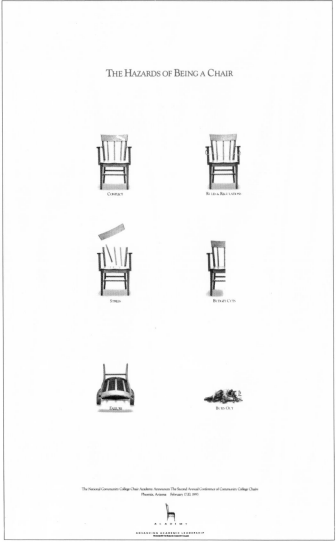

Art Directors/Studio Russ Haan, Brad Smith/After Hours
Designer/Studio Brad Smith/ After Hours
Photographer Art Holeman
Client/Event National Community College Chair Academy, Mesa, AZ/annual international conference
Paper Monadnock Caress Smooth Natural
Colors Two, black and match
Type Frutiger 45, manipulated (logo); Goudy (catalog)

Printing Offset
Initial Print Run 12,000, each poster
Cost $20,000

Concept These posters promote two annual academic chair conferences. Though the themes of the conferences are serious, these posters grab attention by being unexpectedly humorous, which was appreciated by an academic audience unaccustomed to this kind of

approach. The first year of the conference was promoted by the poster "The Trick to Being a Chair," which related to the conference theme of what people need to do to succeed as an academic chair; the second year of the conference was promoted by the poster "The Hazards of Being a Chair," which related to the conference's theme of helping chairs address and overcome obstacles encountered during their jobs.

Cost-Saving Technique The

whole piece is two-color, with black-and-white illustrations.
Distribution of Piece The piece was mailed and handed out at trade shows to deans, academic department chairs, and presidents of community colleges.
Response to Promotion The first year of the conference exceeded attendance goals by 100, to total 600 attendees; the second year, attendance grew to more than 850.

Art Direct[...]
Fisher/Ca[...]
Designer[...]
Brad Smit[...]
Illustrat[...]
Client/Event National
Community College Chair
Academy, Mesa, AZ/annual international conference
Paper Productolith Gloss by
Consolidated
Colors Four, black and match
Type Hand-lettering
Printing Offset
Initial Print Run 12,000
Cost $10,000

Concept This brochure and postcard set uses a whimsical approach to attract academic department chairs to an annual conference. The straightforward theme, "The Characteristics of a Great Chair," is illustrated with a fanciful series of chair-related visual puns that play with the qualities listed in the piece. This approach sets the promotion apart from the seriousness of the typical academic promotion; it actually makes it look like this leadership conference could be fun. It also nicely conveys the point of the conference: the importance of developing a wide variety of personality traits, particularly a sense of humor.

Special Visual Effect An offbeat approach to lettering, including the filling in of the loops, furthers the whimsical look of the piece.

Cost-Saving Technique The brochure was designed so that, with a simple switch in paper stocks during the print run, the piece could be cut up and used as postcards, too.

Distribution of Piece The piece was mailed and distributed at trade shows to academic department chairs, deans, and college and university presidents.

Response to Promotion Initial comments and preregistration indicate the client will meet attendance goals.

~~WER IN~~
~~ERSHIP~~

~~rt~~ Director/Studio Jack Anderson/Hornall Anderson Design Works

Designers/Studio Jack Anderson, Cliff Chung, Scott Eggers, David Bates, Leo Raymundo/Hornall Anderson Design Works

Client/Event Food Services of America, Seattle, WA/annual sales conference

Paper Simpson Starwhite Vicksburg (folder), Tuxedo (invitation), Neenah Classic Crest (stationery)

Colors Six, match (folder); three, match (exhibit); four, match, plus foil (invitation); two, match (name tags)

Type Futura Extra Bold

Printing Screenprinting

Software Aldus FreeHand

Concept This Power in Partnership campaign was developed for the annual sales conference of Food Services of America, an institutional food distributor. The promotion's objective was twofold: to provide a dynamic environment for FSA to reinforce the strength of its position in the food service industry, and to add excitement to the event. The star logo developed for the conference is a visual allusion to FSA's logo; eight additional icons relating to food service, communication, and partnership were developed to support the main logo.

Special Visual Effect Varnishing the "energy burst" pattern on the invitation gives it extra vibrancy.

Cost-Saving Technique The environmental graphics were created from durable components so that FSA would be able to reuse them.

Distribution of Piece The invitation was mailed to FSA sales associates and vendors.

Response to Promotion The promotion succeeded in creating a dynamic working environment for the conference, and Hornall Anderson is now developing graphics for next year's conference.

CHEMICAL FREE WHEELIN'

Art Director/Studio John Sayles/Sayles Graphic Design

Designer/Studio John Sayles/Sayles Graphic Design

Illustrator John Sayles

Client/Event RAGBRAI XX, Des Moines, IA/party connected with bicycle ride

Paper Nekoosa White Opaque Cover

Colors Three, black and match

Type Hand-lettering

Printing Offset (poster), screen-printing (T-shirt)

Initial Print Run 250

Cost None (materials and services donated)

Concept Lively colors and illustrations give excitement to this pro-

motion for an alcohol- and chemical-free party connected with a bike ride event.

Special Visual Effect The bicycle logo on the poster and the front of the T-shirt is repeated, in black-and-white form, on the back of the T-shirt.

Cost-Saving Techniques Paper and printing were donated by local printers; to save on typesetting costs, John Sayles hand-rendered the text for the entire poster.

Distribution of Piece The posters were hand-delivered to local businesses; the T-shirts were handed out to participants in the bike ride.

Response to Promotion The party was well attended.

Art Director/Studio Jack Anderson/Hornall Anderson Design Works

Designers/Studio Jack Anderson, Cliff Chung, David Bates, Leo Raymundo, Brian O'Neill/Hornall Anderson Design Works

Illustrators Scott McDougall, Yataka Sasaki

Client/Event Microsoft Corporation, Redmond, WA/technical conference

Paper Neenah Environment Text, Moonrock (flyers)

Colors Four, black and match

Type Gill Sans, Palatino (flyers)

Printing Offset

Software Aldus FreeHand, Aldus PageMaker (flyers)

Initial Print Run 200,000

Concept Microsoft Corporation needed a logo and collateral materials to promote its technical conference on products supporting Microsoft's Windows platform. The logo incorporates a *T* (technical) and an *E* (education), combined with a column that suggests a strong, stable education. The flyers are functional and easy to follow. Another part of the conference materials was a ball that could be squeezed to reduce stress; a CD including information about the conference was given to some of the participants.

Special Visual Effects The use of bright retro tints on a marbled gray background gives the flyer more vibrancy than the average conference materials. Curved, brightly colored tag lines lead the reader through the brochure.

Distribution of Piece The flyer was mailed before the conference to prospective attendees; other components were given to attendees on arrival.

RUN FOR THE ZOO MARATHON

Art Director/Studio Steve Wedeen/Vaughn Wedeen Creative
Designer/Studio Steve Wedeen/Vaughn Wedeen Creative
Illustrator Kevin Tolman
Client/Event Rio Grande Zoo and Dion's Pizza, Albuquerque, NM/marathon
Paper Simpson Starwhite Vicksburg White Cover
Colors Eight, match
Type Matrix Wide
Printing Silkscreening
Software QuarkXPress
Initial Print Run 250 (large poster); 1,000 (small poster); 5,000 (miscellaneous pieces)

Concept This silkscreened poster, which promotes a marathon bene-

fitting the Rio Grande Zoo, uses a visual pun of a sneaker-clad elephant running. This brightly colored graphic was also adapted for use on T-shirts, advertisements, and other collateral connected to the event.

Cost-Saving Techniques Miscellaneous print collateral was ganged with the poster's press run; Vaughn Wedeen reduced its fees and Dion's Pizza underwrote the event.
Distribution of Piece The poster was primarily sold at the event.

Response to Promotion Recognition of and turnout at the event were very good.

ZOO BOO 4

Art Director/Studio Steve Wedeen/Vaughn Wedeen Creative
Designer/Studio Steve Wedeen/ Vaughn Wedeen Creative
Illustrator Steve Wedeen
Client/Event Rio Grande Zoo, Albuquerque, NM/Zoo Boo Halloween event
Paper Simpson Starwhite Vicksburg Smooth White Cover
Colors Six, black and match
Type Viking, Copperplate
Printing Offset
Software Aldus FreeHand, QuarkXPress
Initial Print Run 1,000

Concept This poster commemorates and promotes an annual Halloween event at the Rio Grande Zoo. The graphic nature and bold colors of the poster set the stage for a fun event that is truly in keeping with Halloween.

Distribution of Piece The poster was hung in windows and in public places two to three weeks before the event; collateral was purchased and distributed at the event itself.
Response to Promotion Turnout at the event was good.

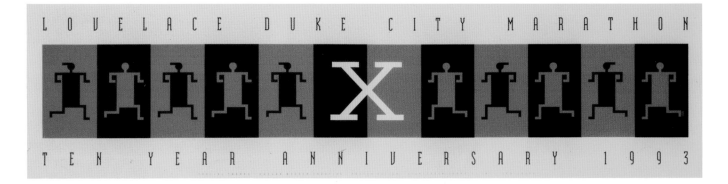

Art Directors/Studio Rick Vaughn, Vicki Newsom/Vaughn Wedeen Creative
Designer/Studio Rick Vaughn/Vaughn Wedeen Creative
Illustrator Chip Wyly
Client/Event Duke City Marathon, Albuquerque, NM/marathon
Paper Arches 88

Colors Three, black and match
Type Lubalin Graph, Modula Serif
Printing Silkscreening
Software Aldus FreeHand
Initial Print Run 90

Concept This poster commemorated the tenth anniversary of the Lovelace Duke City Marathon. The use of the Roman numeral X as the centerpiece, surrounded with ten running figures, communicated the event's tenth anniversary. The bold primary colors and strong horizontal shape ensured that the poster would grab the viewer's attention.
Cost-Saving Technique As a result of budget reductions, only three colors were used for the poster.
Distribution of Piece The poster was sold at the race, as well as given to board members.
Response to Promotion The posters and other materials were a big hit, both with board members and the general public.

Art Director/Studio Rick Vaughn/Vaughn Wedeen Creative
Designer/Studio Rick Vaughn/Vaughn Wedeen Creative
Illustrator Rick Vaughn
Client/Event Duke City Marathon, Albuquerque, NM/marathon
Paper French Speckletone Black Cover
Colors Four, match
Type Matrix Wide
Printing Silkscreening
Software QuarkXPress, Adobe Illustrator
Initial Print Run 150

Concept This poster for the Lovelace Duke City Marathon incorporates brightly colored icons—coyote, yucca, mountains, etc.—that symbolize the New Mexico locale, and combines them with runners to convey the notion of a marathon held in the Southwest.
Distribution of Piece The piece was sold at the event, as well as given to board members.
Response to Promotion The marathon was a great success, attracting one thousand entrants; the poster and collateral materials were also the most popular with the public since the marathon's beginnings in 1984.

REACH FOR THE
STARS

Art Director/Studio John Sayles/Sayles Graphic Design

Designer/Studio John Sayles/Sayles Graphic Design

Illustrator John Sayles

Client/Event Advertising Professionals of Des Moines, Des Moines, IA/annual recognition program

Paper James River Cream/Black Vellum Text (letterhead), James River Black Antique Tuscan Cover (poster)

Colors Two, match (letterhead, sweatshirt); three, match (poster, awards)

Type Hand-tooled (display type), Garamond Bold (body)

Printing Screenprinting (poster, awards, sweatshirt), offset (letterhead)

Initial Print Run 1,000 (posters), 5,000 (letterhead)

Concept This campaign promoted the twenty-fifth anniversary of the

ADDYs, an annual design and advertising recognition program sponsored by the Advertising Professionals of Des Moines. The "Reach for the Stars" theme is echoed by the illustrated woman and by the star motif (twenty-five of which appear on the sweatshirt and letterhead).

Special Visual Effect As a visual accent, the metallic silver underscores the twenty-fifth anniversary nature of the event.

Cost-Saving Techniques Printing was donated by local printers; award and textile materials were provided at cost.

Distribution of Piece Pieces were mailed and hand-delivered to association members and others in the advertising industry several times over a six-month period.

Response to Promotion Nearly four hundred people attended the event, a great increase over past attendance.

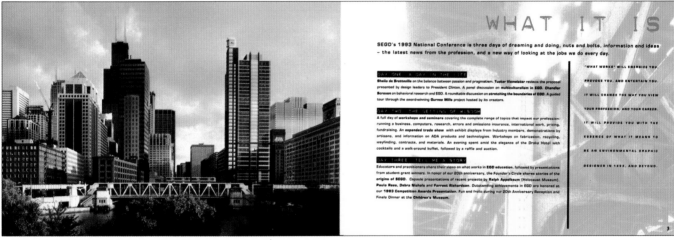

Art Director/Studio Clifford Stoltze/Stoltze Design
Designers/Studio Clifford Stoltze, Peter Farrell, Rebecca Fagan/Stoltze Design
Photographers Greg Hursley, Rudolph Janu, Allan Shortall, Carol Naughton, Barbara Karant
Client/Event Society for Environmental Graphic Design, Cambridge, MA/national conference
Paper Fox River Confetti, Potlatch Vintage Velvet
Colors Two, black and match
Type Engravers Gothic, New Baskerville, Trade Gothic, Trade Gothic Condensed, Avenir, Clarendon, Clarendon Condensed, Monotype Grotesque, Confidential, Karton, Flight Case, Dynamoe, Eurostile, Orator, Futura
Printing Offset
Software Aldus FreeHand, Aldus PageMaker
Initial Print Run 10,200 (booklets); 3,000 (letterhead); 2,000 (#10 envelopes); 1,000 (booklet envelopes); 1,500 (second sheets)
Cost $12,550

Concept This promotion for the nonprofit Society for Environmental Graphic Design's 1993 national conference uses a functional approach, inspired by industrial vernacular design, to underscore the quality of the conference, as well as its theme, "What Works."

Special Visual Effects The "What Works" logo, with its mottled inking and its varied placement throughout conference collateral, has the feel of a rubber stamp—a pragmatic look that suits the theme of the conference. All the other graphic elements in the booklet—the color palette, the gritty photographs, the label-like headings—are also appropriately functional.

Cost-Saving Techniques Printing was limited to two colors, to minimize costs. Stoltze Design donated its services, RIS Paper discounted the cover stock, and the photographers donated photo usage.

Distribution of Piece The piece was mailed once to members of SEGD.

Response to Promotion Attendance at the conference doubled from the previous year.

DALLAS SOCIETY OF VISUAL COMMUNICATIONS

Art Directors/Studio Shawn Freeman, Todd Hart/Focus 2
Designers/Studio Shawn Freeman, Todd Hart/Focus 2
Photographer Duane Michals
Illustrator Duane Michals
Client/Event Dallas Society of Visual Communications, Dallas, TX/speech
Paper Photographic print
Colors One, black
Type Hand-lettering, Adobe Garamond
Printing Photographic
Software QuarkXPress
Initial Print Run 100
Cost None (all materials and services donated)

Concept To commemorate the occasion of photographer Duane Michals speaking to the Dallas Society of Visual Communications, Focus 2 designed this print featuring one of his photographs. The photographer specializes in black-and-white images with text handwritten directly on the print; this print exemplifies his style.
Distribution of Piece The piece

BLACK IS UGLY

was hand-delivered to DSVC members.
Response to Promotion The print generated high interest and participation in the event, as well as about $1,000 revenue.

JAMES LEUNG DESIGN

Art Director/Studio James Wai Mo Leung/James Leung Design
Designer/Studio James Wai Mo Leung/James Leung Design
Client/Event James Leung Design, Brooklyn, NY/design school exhibit
Paper Canson card stock
Colors Three, black and match
Type Caslon 540
Printing Silkscreening
Software QuarkXPress
Initial Print Run 1,000

Concept This individual designer's invitation to the Senior Show at the Parsons School of Design

demonstrates that it's not necessary to be flashy to be creative. The simplicity of the concept and execution—with the black type on black background representing invisibility, and the orange dots representing visibility—is an apt demonstration of the very creativity referred to in the copy.
Distribution of Piece The piece was mailed to friends and potential employers.
Response to Promotion The designer got a freelance position at Pentagram Design shortly after the show.

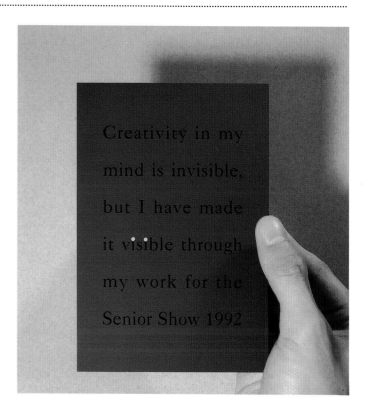

Creativity in my mind is invisible, but I have made it visible through my work for the Senior Show 1992

Art Director/Studio Terry Laurenzio/246 Fifth Design
Designers/Studio Terry Laurenzio, Sid Lee/246 Fifth Design
Illustrator Paula Taaffe
Client/Event The Ottawa International Jazz Festival, Ottawa, Ontario/jazz festival
Paper Eco-Jenson
Colors Four, process, with double-hit of black
Type Bergell, Retro Bold, Univers
Printing Offset
Software Adobe Photoshop, QuarkXPress
Initial Print Run 2,000 (T-shirts), 3,000 (posters), 80,000 (pocket schedules), 300,000 (official programs), 22,000 (passports), 2,000 (postcards), 50 (bus shelter posters)
Cost $25,300 (printing; design and typesetting donated)

Concept This dynamic campaign for an international jazz festival hums with the vitality and spirit of the art form it celebrates. This promotion counteracts Ottawa's reputation for conservatism and suggests the international nature of the event with its vivid color scheme, lively illustration style, and trendy type treatment. The overall impression—of the campaign and of the event itself—is one of quality and sophistication.

Cost-Saving Techniques Artwork was produced on the Macintosh, and pieces were ganged together during the print run. Suppliers produced the pieces at a discount, and design and typesetting were donated.

Distribution of Piece Posters were displayed around the city three weeks prior to the festival, and other components were sold at the festival.

Response to Promotion The festival had a record attendance of 200,000, and all its attendant merchandise sold out.

LEWIS WEDDING

Art Director/Studio Maureen Erbe/Maureen Erbe Design
Designers/Studio Maureen Erbe, Rita A. Sowins/Maureen Erbe Design
Client/Event Marcy and Simon Lewis, Sherman Oaks, CA/wedding
Paper Richard De Bas Floral (exterior), Strathmore Pastelle Natural White Cover (interior)
Colors Three, match
Type Bernhard Tango, Liberty, Gill Sans Bold
Printing Offset
Software QuarkXPress
Initial Print Run 200

Concept This wedding invitation was designed to be a keepsake to commemorate the occasion, as well as a special gift in itself.
Special Visual Effects The piece features a unique paper in which wildflowers are prominent; the blue twine used to bind the piece complements the blue in some of the flowers. The script typefaces give it a lovely traditional feel, but the layering of the type and the unusual ink colors give this type treatment a modern twist.

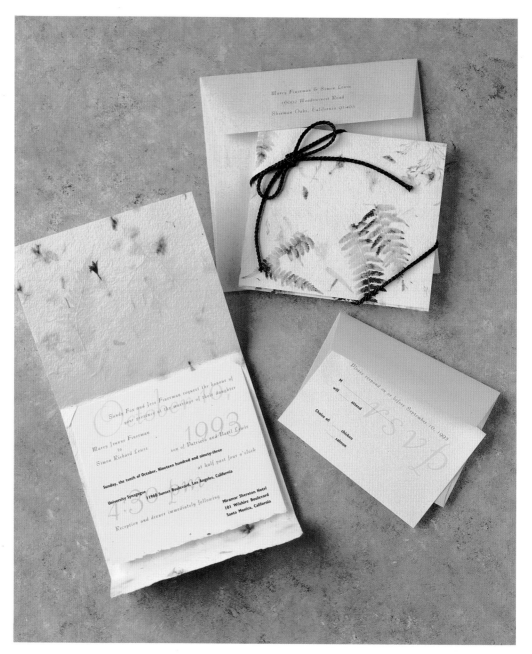

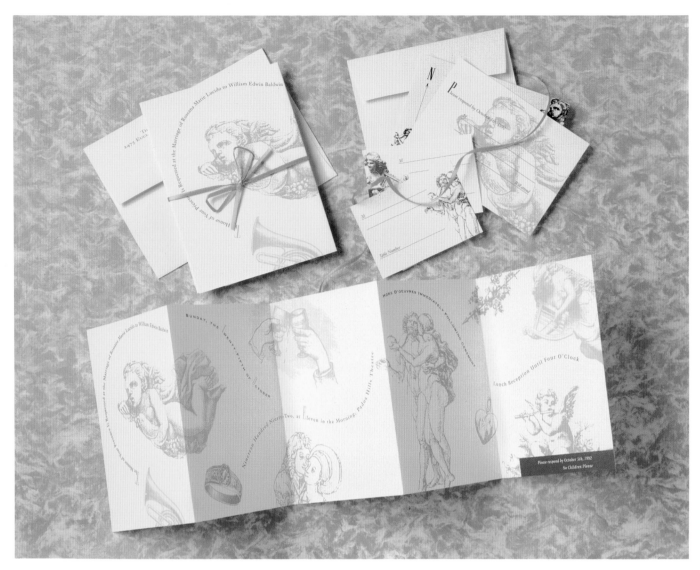

Art Director/Studio Rossana Lucido/Timbuk 2 Design
Designer/Studio Rossana Lucido/Timbuk 2 Design
Client/Event Rossana Lucido and William Baldwin/wedding
Paper Karma Natural, Strathmore Pastel Natural
Colors Three, match
Type Ultra Condensed, Janson, Copperplate

Printing Offset
Software Aldus FreeHand
Initial Print Run 250
Cost $1,100

Concept The designer of this lovely wedding invitation was also the bride. The invitation she created tied into the wedding's Victorian theme with clip art illustrations that have an old-fashioned feel; the antique-looking creme stock and gentle color scheme, as well as the slender pink ribbon that ties it all together, further this motif. However, the foldout brochure format and flowing type treatment give the invitation a contemporary feel.

Cost-Saving Technique The enclosed maps were laser printed by the designer.

DALLAS SOCIETY OF
VISUAL COMMUNICATIONS

Art Directors/Studio Todd Hart, Shawn Freeman/Focus 2

Designers/Studio Todd Hart, Shawn Freeman/Focus 2

Photographer Phil Hollenbeck

Copywriter Bill Baldwin

Client/Event Dallas Society of Visual Communications, Dallas, TX/speech

Colors Four, process

Type Futura

Printing Offset

Software QuarkXPress, Aldus FreeHand, Adobe Photoshop

Initial Print Run 1,500

Cost None (materials and services donated)

Concept To entice DSVC members to attend an event where the creative director of Nike Graphic Design was speaking, Focus 2 came up with this clever invitation. Fittingly, the box the invitation came in is shoelaced together (with a hang-tag that instructs the recipient to "Just undo it"), and the interior copy continues this play on Nike's famous "Just Do It" campaign, both in look and verbal style. The copy ends with the words "Just go to it," and the enclosed T-shirt reinforces this message by including a version of this slogan that incorporates the DSVC logo. The ingenuity and high level of interactivity of this invitation ensured that it—and the event it promoted— would be remembered.

Special Visual Effects The top and bottom interior borders of the box are die-cut, and the top and the bottom sides of the box include the words "Do it." In keeping with the irreverent tone of the piece, the cover sneaker is a Nike "air huarache."

Distribution of Piece The piece was mailed once to DSVC members.

Response to Promotion Turnout at the event was substantial.

Art Director/Studio Kit Hinrichs/Pentagram Design
Designer/Studio Catherine Wong/Pentagram Design
Photographer Terry Heffernan
Client/Event Simpson Paper Company, San Francisco, CA/design competition
Paper Simpson Starwhite Vicksburg, Tiara, Vellum
Colors One, match, and four, process
Type Gill Sans
Printing Offset
Initial Print Run 60,000

Concept A photograph of an elegant "assemblage" of Simpson paper was an appropriate centerpiece for this campaign, which promoted a design competition sponsored by Simpson. The almost abstract nature of this collage was an ideal way to appeal to a diverse audience and to solicit a broad range of entries for the competition.

Distribution of Piece The call for entries was distributed through direct mail and through paper distributors to designers, printers and print buyers; awards were distributed to winners in the competition.

Response to Promotion The call for entries resulted in an increased number of entries, including a greater number of international entries, over previous years.

CONSTRUCTING IOWA'S FUTURE

Art Director/Studio John Sayles/
Sayles Graphic Design

Designer/Studio John Sayles/
Sayles Graphic Design

Illustrator John Sayles

Client/Event Associated General
Contractors of Iowa, Des Moines,
IA/annual convention

Paper Kraft (poster), chipboard
(brochure cover), Astrobright
Goldenrod (brochure text)

Colors Three, black and match

Type Hand-lettering (headline),
typewritten (text)

Printing Screenprinting (poster,
brochure cover), offset (brochure
text)

Initial Print Run 600
(brochures), 200 (posters)

Concept "Constructing Iowa's
Future" was the theme of the annual convention of the Associated
General Contractors, as well as the
theme of this promotion. This
theme was carried out in the use of
industrial materials like chipboard,
kraft paper and staples to create
an appropriately rustic, masculine
promotion. Invitation information
is included on a 2-by-3½-inch booklet stapled to the die-cut brochure
"cover."

Special Visual Effects The booklet text is typewritten, in keeping
with the utilitarian bent of this
promotion. The piece is die-cut in
such a way that, when freestanding
on its side, the illustrated worker
looks through his telescope at the
text of the booklet.

Cost-Saving Technique Costs
were cut by selecting industrial
paper and by using screenprinting
instead of offset for the small print
run of posters and brochure covers.

Distribution of Piece The piece
was mailed once to association
members.

Response to Promotion
Attendance goals for the event
were exceeded.

CLARK'S OF ENGLAND

Art Director/Studio Kit Hinrichs/Pentagram Design
Designer/Studio Kit Hinrichs/ Pentagram Design
Client/Event Clark's of England/ presentation of new line of shoes
Initial Print Run 50

Concept To introduce a new line of Clark's shoes for women to an American audience, saucers with the Clark's logo were hand-delivered to a select group of department store buyers; to receive the matching cup (and a bonus of tea bags), the buyers had to attend a special presentation of the new line. This promotion effectively conveyed the quality of the British line of shoes, as well as providing incentive for buyers to attend the presentation.

Cost-Saving Techniques Because the size of the promotion was limited, the purchase of expensive tea sets placed in standard boxes with two-color printed invitations made an inexpensive promotion look expensive.

Distribution of Piece The piece was hand-delivered once to major department store shoe buyers two weeks prior to the event.

Response to Promotion Clark's got nearly 100 percent attendance at the presentation.

LOW-BUDGET PROMOTIONAL AND SELF-PROMOTIONAL PIECES

Art Director/Studio José Serrano/Mires Design

Designers/Studio José Serrano, David Fielding/Mires Design

Illustrators Jennifer Hewitson, Tuko Fujisaki, Debbie Tilley, Randy Verougstraete

Client/Service Joined at the Hip, Cardiff, CA/illustration

Paper Carolina Coated Cover

Colors Four, process, and two, match, plus varnish

Type Various

Printing Offset

Software Adobe Illustrator

Initial Print Run 3,000

Cost None (illustration was traded for design, color separation and printing services)

Concept This deck of playing cards serves as an enjoyable and convenient portfolio of the work of four freelance illustrators. Each illustrator was assigned a different suit to interpret as he or she saw fit; the back of the cards include the Joined at the Hip logo and the names and phone numbers of all of the illustrators. The box gives the credit information, so art directors will know which illustrator was assigned to each suit. This ingenious format is one that's portable (the cards measure a mere 2½-by-3½-inches) and cost-efficient, as well as fun and useful for its recipients.

Special Visual Effect Each of the four sides of the box includes the name of one of the illustrators and the symbol of the suit he or she illustrated.

Distribution of Piece The piece was advertised and offered free to art directors who sent in their business cards; it was mailed once to the existing mailing list, as well as in response to requests.

Response to Promotion The firm was able to build a focused mailing list, and all of the illustrators received a number of projects that could be directly traced to the promotion.

COPYRIGHT/COPYWRONG
SEMINAR

Art Director/Studio Dave
Webster/Webster Design
Associates, Inc.
Designer/Studio Dave Webster/
Webster Design Associates, Inc.
Illustrator Dave Webster
Client/Event The American
Institute of Graphic Arts, Omaha,
NE/copyright law seminar
Paper Various
Colors One, black
Type Helvetica Inserat (head-
ings), Helvetica Condensed Light
(body)
Printing Offset
Software Aldus FreeHand
Initial Print Run 2,500
Cost None (materials and ser-
vices donated)

Concept To promote an AIGA
seminar on copyright law (entitled
"Copyright/Copywrong"), this campaign, with its use of reverse and
upside-down type and graphics,
plays on the idea of opposites. The
copyright symbol is incorporated
into both the 22-by-22-inch poster
invitation and the 6-by-6-inch
deadline extension mailer in a
number of clever ways, including
as an eye on the poster's happy
face ("Copyright") and sad face
("Copywrong").
Cost-Saving Techniques One-
color printing helped keep costs
down. The studio used a variety of
uncoated papers that the paper
company had in stock, and AIGA
volunteers did the folding and
mailing. All materials and services
were donated.
Distribution of Piece The initial
poster invitation was mailed once
to area designers and advertising
professionals; this was followed
with a second mailing of the smaller deadline extension piece.
Response to Promotion In spite
of heavy snow the day of the seminar, seventy-five people attended,
and AIGA raised $4,000.

Art Director/Studio Rick Tharp/
Tharp Did It

Designers/Studio Rick Tharp,
Colleen Sullivan/Tharp Did It

Client/Service Tharp Did It, Los
Gatos, CA/graphic design

Paper Simpson EverGreen
Recycled

Colors One, black

Type Courier (from an old Royal
typewriter)

Printing Silkscreening, thermography (business card)

Print Run 200

Cost $127.50

Concept In the January/February
1993 issue of *Communication Arts*
magazine, an article by Rick Tharp
described a conversation a member
of his staff had with a printer about
a business card order. The order—
for a tongue-in-cheek version of the
studio's card calling the business
"poodle grooming, repair, taxidermy
and graphic design," complete with
illustrations of a poodle and a chain
saw—confused every department

at the printing company. The article recounted every humorous, and
frustrating, detail of the phone conversation that resulted. After the
article appeared, Tharp's office
received many requests for a copy
of the business card that caused all
the fuss, and he designed this
poster as a vehicle to distribute the
cards. The poster is uncluttered by
graphics, so nothing will interfere
with the story it tells; its only
graphic is the business card itself, a
copy of which is actually attached

to the poster.

Cost-Saving Technique The text
was typewritten on an old Royal
typewriter and enlarged on a photocopier.

Distribution of Piece The piece
was mailed to those who requested
a copy of the business card after
they saw Tharp's article in
Communication Arts; now people
are calling to request the poster
itself.

SEGURA INC.

Art Director/Studio Carlos Segura/Segura Inc.

Designer/Studio Carlos Segura/Segura Inc.

Illustrator Carlos Segura

Client/Service Segura Inc., Chicago, IL/graphic design

Paper Wyndstone Fascade

Colors Two, black and match

Type Typewriter

Printing Offset

Software QuarkXPress, Adobe Illustrator, Superpaint, Streamline

Initial Print Run 1,000

Concept This simple postcard promotion gives thirteen examples of Segura Inc.'s logo work in an efficient six-by-nine-inch space. The logos are accompanied by copy that indirectly sells the studio's design services by selling the importance of good design.

Special Visual Effect The oversized return address also serves as the necessary contact information, so the other side of the card doesn't have to be cluttered with more information.

Cost-Saving Techniques The postcard format cuts down on postage and paper costs; two-color printing also keeps costs down.

Distribution of Piece The piece was mailed to clients and potential clients.

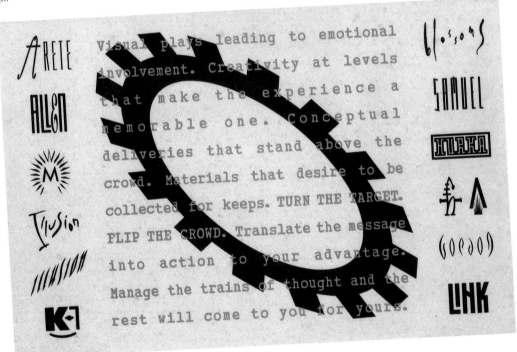

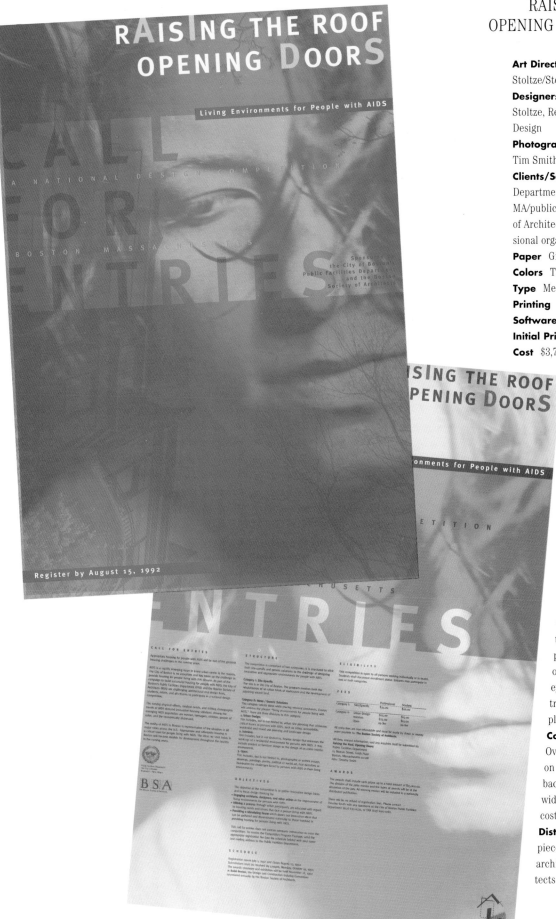

Art Director/Studio Clifford Stoltze/Stoltze Design

Designers/Studio Clifford Stoltze, Rebecca Fagan/Stoltze Design

Photographers Rebecca Fagan, Tim Smith

Clients/Services Public Facilities Department of Boston, Boston, MA/public service; Boston Society of Architects, Boston, MA/professional organization

Paper Gilbert ESSE

Colors Three and two, match

Type Meta

Printing Offset

Software Aldus FreeHand

Initial Print Run 5,000

Cost $3,703

Concept This piece is a call for entries for a competition to design living environments for people with AIDS. The flyer's unusual format and color palette ensured that it would stand out in a stack of mail.

Special Visual Effect The graphics on the front of the piece consist primarily of two photographs superimposed, with the back being a tint of just one of the photographs; yet the use of ink and an unusual, eye-catching typographic treatment give the piece plenty of graphic impact.

Cost-Saving Technique Overprinting three colors on the front and two on the back gives the effect of a wider color palette for less cost.

Distribution of Piece The piece was mailed once to architects, landscape architects and students.

DAY OF THE DEAD

Art Directors/Studio Eric and Jackson Boelts/Boelts Bros. Design
Designers/Studio Kerry Stratford, Eric and Jackson Boelts/Boelts Bros. Design
Illustrators Kerry Stratford, Eric and Jackson Boelts
Client/Service Tucson Arts Coalition, Tucson, AZ/arts association
Paper Champion Kromekote
Colors Three, match
Type Glypha
Printing Silkscreening
Software Aldus FreeHand
Initial Print Run 100
Cost $500

Concept This poster uses an eye-catching visual of costumed skeletons to promote a Halloween costume party with a Mexican "Day of the Dead" theme.
Special Visual Effect Subtle details like the use of copper metallic ink and spot varnishes, and the carrying out of the bone motif in the poster's lettering, make sure this poster gets a second look.
Distribution of Piece Posters were hung in retail spaces in downtown Tucson.
Response to Promotion The party was a hit, and the arts coalition met its fund-raising goals for the event.

BOELTS BROS. DESIGN

Art Directors/Studio Jackson and Eric Boelts, Kerry Stratford/Boelts Bros. Design
Designers/Studio Jackson and Eric Boelts, Kerry Stratford/Boelts Bros. Design
Client/Service Boelts Bros. Design, Tucson, AZ/graphic design
Paper Champion Kromekote
Colors Two, match
Type Helvetica Bold Condensed
Printing Offset
Software Aldus FreeHand
Initial Print Run 300
Cost $600

Concept This poster demonstrates the impact of a strong concept executed simply. Designed as a response to violence in Bosnia and in Los Angeles, this poster employs an iconic human figure on a vibrant background to convey its thoughtful message.
Special Visual Effect Split-fountain printing of orange and yellow ink gives the poster the feel of a sunrise—a feeling that reinforces the poster's message of hope.
Distribution of Piece The piece was mailed over a three-month period to friends, clients, students and Los Angeles agencies.
Response to Promotion The studio received a lot of positive verbal feedback, and the poster still hangs on many of the recipients' walls.

Art Directors/Studio Craig Bernhardt, Janice Fudyma/ Bernhardt Fudyma Design Group
Designers/Studio Iris Brown, Jane Sobczak, Ignacio Rodriguez/Bernhardt Fudyma Design Group
Photographers Earl Ripling, Dennis Gottlieb
Client/Service Bernhardt Fudyma Design Group, New York, NY/graphic design
Paper Various, as available; vellum interleaf
Colors Four, process
Type New Baskerville, Helvetica Condensed
Printing Offset
Software QuarkXPress
Initial Print Run Created on an as-needed basis

Concept This 6-by-6-inch portfolio consists of the trimmed-off portions of clients' print jobs, which the design firm utilized (with clients' permission) to print photographs of its work. Bernhardt Fudyma interspersed these pages with vellum interleaf pages, which provided the necessary explanation for projects presented in the booklet.
Special Visual Effect Photographs of projects are printed on a wide variety of papers; some of the pages fold out to showcase special projects.
Special Production Technique The studio used its own mini wiro binding machine to assemble brochures as necessary, in any combination of pages desired.
Cost-Saving Technique Production cost was limited to the cost of separations, extra stripping and trimming.
Distribution of Piece The piece was distributed by mail and as leave-behinds to potential and existing clients.
Response to Promotion The response has been overwhelmingly positive.

...SHER

...io Carolyn Fisher/Carolyn

... Peter Shikany/P.S. Studios
...n Fisher

Client/Service Carolyn Fisher, New York, NY/illustration

Paper Warren Lustro Dull Creme Cover
Colors Four, process
Type Hand-lettering
Printing Offset
Initial Print Run 500
Cost None (materials and services donated)

Concept This 11-by-17-inch poster, inspired by G.K. Chesterton's quotation, "Angels can fly because they take themselves lightly," was appropriately themed for the holiday season. However, the poster's gentle sentiment and subtle execution make it a refreshing change from the usual holiday promotion.

Cost-Saving Techniques Design was donated by P.S. Studios, printing was donated by Ben Franklin Press, and color separations were donated by Tru Colour.

Distribution of Piece The piece was mailed at Christmas to clients and friends.

DARREL KOLOSTA

Art Director Darrel Kolosta
Designer Darrel Kolosta
Illustrator Darrel Kolosta
Client/Service Darrel Kolosta, Oakland, CA/illustration

Paper Karma Cover
Colors Two, match
Type Futura Book
Printing Offset
Initial Print Run 3,000

Concept This brochure provides a cost-effective way for this illustrator to show off past work. Warmth is added to the simple design by printing the illustrations with a pale yellow background.

Cost-Saving Technique The use of rubber stamps for the purple pencils on the cover gave the piece additional color for little cost.

Distribution of Piece The piece was mailed over a three-month period to design firms and agency and magazine art directors.

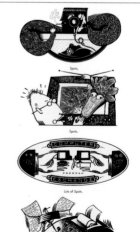

The Columbus Recreation And Parks Department Presents Over 200 Free Outdoor Performances. All In Our Columbus Parks From May 22 Through September 18, 1992. For Further Information Call 645-7995. For Performance Listings Call At 645-3800. It's Quite An Uplifting Experience!

MUSIC IN THE AIR

Art Director/Studio Eric Rickabaugh/ Rickabaugh Graphics

Designer/Studio Eric Rickabaugh/Rickabaugh Graphics

Illustrator Eric Rickabaugh/ Rickabaugh Graphics

Client/Service Department of Parks and Recreation, City of Columbus, Columbus, OH/Music in the Air performance series

Paper Mead Moistrite Matte Cover

Colors Two, match, and four, process

Type Linoscript (text), Futura (schedule), hand-lettering (head)

Printing Offset

Software Adobe Photoshop, Aldus FreeHand

Initial Print Run 1,500

Cost $1,000 (most of costs donated)

Concept As in past "Music in the Air" concert series promotions, this year's poster revolved around a visual play on the series name—this year, by depicting a neoclassical heroic figure holding aloft a musical note. This 14½-by-32½-inch poster serves as both an intriguing promotion of the event and an elegant commemorative piece. It also fulfills the more utilitarian purpose of including all concert site and time information, but it does so unobtrusively, as an inconspicuous yet legible border to the piece.

Special Visual Effect The unusual combination of gold and copper metallic inks gives the poster subtle visual flair.

Cost-Saving Techniques The entire piece was created on the computer and output as separated film, to eliminate typesetting and stripping charges. Design, illustration, film separation output and paper were donated; printing was provided at a discount.

Distribution of Piece The piece was hand-delivered over a three-month period to various public sites and private businesses.

MAN

AIR

Irena Roman

lyn Albert

a Roman

Client/Service Irena Roman,
Scituate, MA/illustration

Paper Golden Cask Cover (folder), Text (inserts)

Colors One, black

Type Bodoni Light

Printing Offset

Software QuarkXPress

Initial Print Run 1,000

Cost $2,460

Concept The illustrator's graphite drawings of celebrities, which originally appeared in *The New Yorker*, were meant to be seen one at a time. This mailer allows for this,

yet it also makes a cohesive statement about the illustrator's work. The final effect is of a gallery of miniature movie posters.

Cost-Saving Techniques The designer donated her services. Printing the piece in one color helped keep costs down.

Distribution of Piece The piece was sporadically mailed in batches of one hundred to art directors and art buyers.

Response to Promotion Because the appeal of the subject matter was universal, the piece was viewed as a keepsake by many of its recipients. It has generated $10,000 worth of assignments for the illustrator.

TRIMARK FURNITURE

Art Director/Studio Toni
Schowalter/Schowalter 2 Design

Designer/Studio Toni
Schowalter/Schowalter 2 Design

Photographer Thomas Brummett

Client/Product TriMark
Furniture, Philadelphia, PA/fine
furniture

Paper Potlatch Vintage Velvet
(cards), Simpson EverGreen
Spruce (folder)

Colors Two, black and match

Type Bodoni Bold, Helvetica Bold

Printing Offset

Software QuarkXPress

Initial Print Run 3,000

Cost $6,000

Concept This clever and versatile postcard promotion for a fine furniture maker takes an unusual approach to presenting the company's products. Presenting each piece of furniture on a separate

black-and-white card, with copy on the back of the card, accentuates the furniture's status as fine art and sets this promotion apart from the usual catalog format. The postcard format also enables consumers to mix and match various pieces of furniture to more easily visualize

how pieces might work together.

Cost-Saving Techniques The postcards were ganged with the company's business cards to save printing costs and to eliminate paper waste. This format allows the designer to easily add cards for new pieces or take out cards for pieces

that have been discontinued, without reprinting the whole promotion.

Distribution of Piece The piece was distributed at an open house to designers and end users, and has since been mailed and handed out by sales representatives.

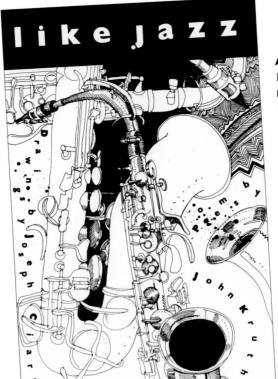

like jazz

Drawings by Joseph Ciardiello

poems by John Kruth

Art Director/Studio Pa[...]
Design
Designer/Studio Patric[...]
Design
Illustrator Joe Ciardiello
Poet John Kruth
Client/Service Joe Ciardiello, Staten Island,
NY/illustration
Paper Warren Lustro Dull Creme Text
Colors One, black
Type Gill Sans, Gill Sans Bold
Printing Offset
Initial Print Run 1,000
Cost $3,000

Concept This book, entitled *Like Jazz*, features illustrations and poetry inspired by a cross section of jazz greats and insiders, such as John Coltrane, Charles Mingus and Billie Holiday. The poems and line drawings interpret the work and personalities of these masters with fitting spontaneity, rhythm and wit.

Cost-Saving Techniques Art and copies of the book were traded for design services. Printing the piece in one color and staple-stitching it, instead of having it perfect-bound, also helped keep costs down.

Distribution of Piece A limited number were sold; some were given out, and some were distributed to magazines, book publishers, design firms and record companies.

Response to Promotion The piece gained the illustrator some new clients and gave him exposure through the book's acceptance in annuals.

Swingin' Be-Bopp circa 195[...]

miles

miles' midnight desire

don't give me any excuses
or a cup of alphabet soup
there's nothin' on tv
and your mom won't be home 'til one

why don't I plug in my trumpet?
you can swim the sidestroke
around the moon
while I pound the voodoo
through your veins
and make you moan
like a bloodhound in heat
and never stop
    and never stop
        and never stop
            to say I'm sorry

PRAHM

Art Director/Studio Richard Prahm/Richard Prahm Design

Illustrator Richard Prahm

Client/Service Richard Prahm Design, San Francisco, CA/design and illustration

Paper Simpson Quest

Colors Two, black and match

Type Compadre, Futura

Printing Laser printing (hang-tag, greeting), screenprinting (T-shirt)

Software Fontographer, QuarkXPress

Initial Print Run 100

Cost $350

Concept This T-shirt promotion takes advantage of an unusual holiday—the Mexican Los Dias de Muertos, or Days of the Dead—as a chance to promote the work of this designer/illustrator. Inspired by his interest in Mexican art and culture, his illustration—a skeleton wear-

ing a sombrero on a motorcycle—is intriguing and memorable, and will certainly lure recipients into reading the explanatory hang-tag.

Special Production Techniques The hang-tag was cut with pinking shears for a distinctive look. The designer's contact information was simply printed out separately and taped onto the interior of the hang-tag.

Cost-Saving Technique The hang-tag and greeting were laser printed.

Distribution of Piece The piece was mailed once to local designers, studios and prospective clients; it was followed up with letters.

STEELHAUS DESIGN

Art Director/Studio Richard L. Smith/Steelhaus Design

Designer/Studio Richard L. Smith/Steelhaus Design

Client/Service Steelhaus Design, Chattanooga, TN/graphic design

Paper French Speckletone Kraft

Colors One, black

Type Helvetica Ultra Compressed, Flintstone, Industria

Printing Laser printing

Software Aldus FreeHand

Initial Print Run 8

Cost $40

Concept This promotion consists of a white box whose lid bears a mysterious black-and-white graphic. Opened, the box reveals a booklet on the history of voodoo. Underneath the booklet is a voodoo doll, and at the bottom of the box

are the words "Hire me or else!" with the designer's name and phone number. The concept was inspired by an old episode of "Dennis the Menace"—and the designer's need for a self-promotional piece.

Cost-Saving Techniques The

booklets were laser printed and hand-bound with twine; the dolls were also handmade. The designer got the boxes from a gift shop.

Distribution of Piece The piece was designed to be mailed to a potential employer after an

interview.

Response to Promotion The only one the designer ever actually sent resulted in a job offer; the rest of the pieces are being saved to follow up future interviews.

Art Dire
Sealock/

Designe
Maverick

Illustra

Client/Service Rick Sealock,
Calgary, Alberta/illustration

Paper Luna Gloss Coated
Recycled

Colors Four, process

Type Various

Printing Offset

Initial Print Run 500 (illustrator), 11,500 (*Studio Magazine*)

Cost $1,500 (Canadian)

Concept The disparate moods of
the editorial illustrations in this
piece demonstrate the range of
conceptual illustration Sealock can
render. The playful use of typography and photocopied spot illustration, as well as the masking tape
that holds the piece together, both
complement Sealock's unique illustration style and reflect his personality.

Distribution of Piece The piece
originated as a one-page ad in
*Studio Magazine's Creative
Directory Annual*; 11,500 copies of
the annual were distributed by the
magazine to designers, art directors, ad agencies, illustrators and
photographers. The illustrator him-
self mailed another five hundred
copies of the tear sheet to his mailing list of editorial, advertising and
publishing clients.

Response to Promotion The
piece immediately brought the
illustrator editorial work and got
his work noticed by advertising art
directors; to date he can trace
$10,000 to $15,000 worth of rev-
enue to this piece.

Designer/Studio Jennifer Dowdell/Full Circle Advertising & Design

Illustrator Jennifer Dowdell

Client/Service Full Circle Advertising & Design, Kenmore, NY/graphic design and promotional advertising

Paper Swiss Imported Thinplate (cover), Neenah Classic Crest Earthstone (interior)

Colors One, black, and hand-coloring

Type Snell Roundhand (initial caps), Palatino (text)

Printing Offset (cover), photo-copying (interior)

Software QuarkXPress

Initial Print Run Photocopied as needed (so far, fewer than 100)

Cost $1.20 each

Concept This booklet plays off the name of the design firm by using the concept of circles. The left-hand page of each spread contains a circular illustration; the right-hand page contains copy that links the illustration to the professional-ism and expertise of Full Circle. The booklet's continued emphasis on the company's name is an appro-priate approach for a start-up com-pany that is trying to establish an identity for itself.

Special Visual Effects Illustra-tions are accented with buttons, pennies and hand-coloring. Vellum was used for the cover, so the found art on the first page could be seen with and without the booklet name.

Cost-Saving Techniques The booklet was reproduced by high-quality photocopiers rather than offset printing, with the designer getting two pages of the booklet out of each 8½-by-11-inch sheet. Paper was bought directly from the dis-tributor. The booklets were colored, cut and bound by hand.

Distribution of Piece The piece was mailed to local businesses as requested.

Response to Promotion Recipients have been delighted with the piece; most have saved them, and some have even request-ed second copies.

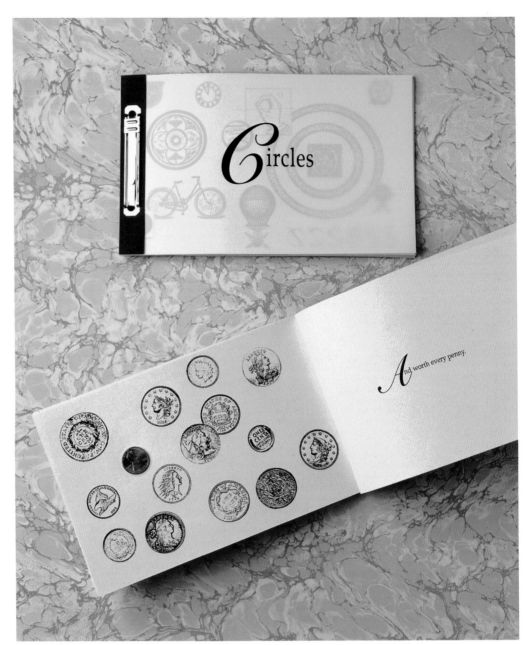

BOELTS BRO[...]
DESIGN

Art Di[...]
Lambe[...]

Designer
Lambe[...]
Design

Photog[...]
Tom Springer, Richard Reens,
Jaime Kuehnel

Illustrator Christie Lambert

Client/Service Lambert Design
Studio, Dallas, TX/graphic design

Paper Black Speckletone (covers,
inside pages), UV Ultra II (inside
pages), Red Brite Hue (flysheets
and bands)

Colors Two, black and match

Type Nofret

Printing Offset thermography
(cover)

Software Adobe Illustrator,
QuarkXPress

Initial Print Run 500

Cost $987

Concept The theme of this self-
promotional booklet is "Eye to i";
the cover features a thermo-
graphed "eye"—the window
through which design is experienced—and each vellum page features an "i" adjective that describes
the studio's work. Also on each vellum page is information about the
project on the page following it.

Cost-Saving Techniques Color
copies were used for photographs
instead of four-color printing; the
booklets were hand-assembled and
bound in-house.

Distribution of Piece The piece
was distributed in a mass mailing,
primarily to prospects and to
clients who hadn't used the studio's services recently. This was
followed by hand-distribution at
meetings.

Response to Promotion The
piece garnered the studio some
new clients, who were impressed
by the studio's ability to come up
with a high-impact, low-cost promotion.

Directors/Studio Eric and Jackson Boelts/Boelts Bros. Design

Designers/Studio Kerry Stratford, Eric and Jackson Boelts/Boelts Bros. Design

Clients/Services Carol Boelts/cooking; Boelts Bros. Design/graphic design

Paper French Speckletone

Colors One, match

Type Baskerville

Printing Offset

Software Aldus PageMaker

Initial Print Run 500

Cost $1,000

Concept This promotion conveys the spirit of Boelts Bros. Design in an inviting, useful and cost-effective format: a collection of cards featuring their mother's recipes. The cards are bound together with a screw that's easy to remove; they are a standard three-by-five-inch size, so recipients can detach the screw and insert the cards in their existing recipe files.

Special Visual Effect The motif of double-themed logos that recurs throughout the studio's self-promotional pieces appears in this piece too: The back of each recipe card is printed with one of these logos, and each category of recipe has an appropriate logo distinguishing it on the top right-hand front corner of each recipe.

Cost-Saving Techniques The whole booklet was printed in one color, and the booklets were collated in-house.

Distribution of Piece The piece was given to friends and sold at stores.

Response to Promotion The promotion generated interviews and newspaper articles about the Boelts brothers and their mother.

Art Directors/Studio Eric and Jackson Boelts/Boelts Bros. Design
Designers/Studio Kerry Stratford, Michele Ramirez, Todd Fedell, Bob Case/Boelts Bros. Design
Client/Service Boelts Bros. Design, Tucson, AZ/graphic design
Paper Neenah Environment
Colors Four, match
Type Baskerville, Gill Sans
Printing Offset
Software Aldus PageMaker, Aldus FreeHand
Initial Print Run 500
Cost $3,000

Concept This thirty-six-page perfect-bound booklet shows off the studio's logo work in a traditional yet slightly off-center way. Each page displays one logo, with a small caption at the bottom explaining the project. In spite of the simplicity of its design, the booklet is kept from looking stark with a variety of warm yet subtle background tones, as well as the use of dark purple ink and recycled paper.
Special Visual Effect The booklet is enclosed in a creme cover die-cut with the studio's logo, which shows off the cover's slate blue interior. The bottom of each page also includes one of the double-themed logos that recurs throughout the studio's self-promotional pieces.
Distribution of Piece The piece was hand-distributed to clients.

FIREHOUSE 101
DESIGN

Art Director/Studio Kirk Richard Smith/Firehouse 101 Design
Designer/Studio Kirk Richard Smith/Firehouse 101 Design
Illustrator Kirk Richard Smith
Client/Service Firehouse 101 Design, Columbus, OH/graphic design and illustration
Paper Potlatch Vintage Gloss
Colors Four, black and match
Type Hand-lettering
Printing Offset
Initial Print Run 1,500
Cost $3,000

Concept The original illustration for this poster, "Smoke and Mirrors," was inspired by the government's lack of response to the AIDS crisis; the rest of the illustrations were built around the themes of "compassion" and "life." The illustrations were used in this poster, as well as a postcard and a booklet format.

Distribution of Piece The promotion was mailed in postcard form weekly for twelve weeks to record companies and magazines; the poster was also used as a leave-behind.

Response to Promotion The promotion garnered the illustrator interest from record companies, as well as magazine work, and has brought in $2,500 in revenue so far.

Art Director/Studio Juliette Borda/Juliette Borda Illustration
Designer/Studio Juliette Borda/Juliette Borda Illustration
Illustrator Juliette Borda
Client/Service Juliette Borda Illustration, Pittsburgh, PA/illustration
Paper Neenah Environment Moonrock
Colors One, black
Type Fashion (cover); Copperplate, Century Old Style (credits)
Printing Photocopying
Initial Print Run 150
Cost $330

Concept The theme "Black and white and seen all over" is appropriate for this illustrator, who wanted to get more work for newspapers.

Special Visual Effect The piece imitates the look of a newspaper in its use of black-and-white ink and grayish, speckled paper that resembles newsprint in look, if not weight.

Cost-Saving Techniques The illustrator used a photocopier to print the booklet and a sewing machine to bind its pages.

Distribution of Piece The piece was mailed once to art directors at newspapers.

Response to Promotion The illustrator heard from a few clients she hadn't worked with in a while, as well as a few new ones; so far, it has brought in $1,890 of work for her.

o William
ter Design
William
Reuter, Jose Bila Rodriguez,
Michael Bain/William Reuter
Design
Photographers Various
Client/Service William Reuter
Design, San Francisco, CA/graphic
design
Paper Pressboard (cover),
Neenah UV Ultra (title pages),
French Speckletone True White
(text)
Colors Four, process, and one,
match
Type Bodoni, Bodoni Italic (text);
typewriter (title pages)
Printing Offset
Software QuarkXPress
Initial Print Run 750

Concept The theme of this portfolio booklet was "work": presentation of the studio's work, design that works. Inspired by industrial manuals from the forties, the booklet employs materials that pick up on this theme.
Special Visual Effect The front cover is die-cut to reveal both the word *works* on the title vellum page, and a fragment of the graphic from the page following the title page.
Special Production Techniques Each piece can be custom-made for recipients, to target their special needs.
Cost-Saving Techniques Recycled file folders were used for the cover, and the piece was bound in-house with Chicago screws; much of the booklet is printed in one color, to help control costs.
Distribution of Piece The piece was distributed both through the mail and as a leave-behind to potential and existing clients.
Response to Promotion The piece got the firm excellent results, with many new clients and projects coming its way.

AFTER HOURS

Art Director/Studio Russ Haan/
After Hours
Designer/Studio Brad Smith/
After Hours
Client/Service After Hours,
Phoenix, AZ/graphic design
Paper Torn moving boxes
Type Helvetica (stamps), hand-lettering
Printing Hand-stamping
Initial Print Run 150
Cost $75

Concept This moving notice came about when the design firm was given thirty days' notice to vacate its old space and find a temporary home; after moving, they realized they had forgotten to tell anyone, so they utilized their empty moving boxes to devise these clever, cost-efficient moving notices.
Cost-Saving Technique The only cost of the piece, besides postage, was the two rubber stamps the designers had made for the piece.
Distribution of Piece The piece was mailed to clients and vendors.

The Institute of Contemporary Art

in conjunction with **The Boston Center for the Arts** *and the exhibition*

El Corazón Sangrante / The Bleeding Heart

presents

POSADA / PROCESIÓN NAVIDEÑA

FREE / GRATIS

Sunday / Domingo

December 15

1991

PRIMERA PARADA

Institute of Contemporary Art
955 Boylston Street, Boston

2:00 p.m.

SEGUNDA PARADA

Centro Cultural Jorge Hernández
85 West Newton Street, Boston

3:00 p.m.

ÚLTIMA PARADA Y FIESTA

Cyclorama
Boston Center for the Arts
539 Tremont Street, Boston

4:00 p.m.

puertas abiertas a las tres

FIESTA NAVIDEÑA

de 4:00 — 7:00 p.m.

Maríachi Guadalajara

Ballet Folklorico "Xochipilli"

Teatro Escena Latina

Aguinaldos y Música Navideña Latino Americana

Parranda

Todos invitados a participar. Llame a **617 266-5151** para más informacion

FREEZING RAIN/BLIZZARD: Reúnase en el Cyclorama a las 3:00 p.m.

El Corazón Sangrante / The Bleeding Heart
was organized by
The Institute of Contemporary Art, Boston.

This exhibition has been made
possible by a major grant from the
Lila Wallace-Reader's Digest Fund.

Additional support has been provided by AT&T,
whose grant has funded in part
a series of international exhibitions; Ellen Poss;
the National Endowment for the Arts,
a federal agency; and
Real Colegio Complutense, Inc.

Special thanks to American Airlines,
Impullsos Bericeos En Accion, Aldus Press
and to Gregorio Rivera and Angelica Ruiz
for their artistic guidance and contribution.

Printing was made possible
through a generous contribution by
Digital Equipment Corporation.

Art Director/Studio Clifford
Stoltze/Stoltze Design
Designer/Studio Clifford Stoltze/
Stoltze Design
Client/Service Institute of
Contemporary Art, Boston, MA/art
museum
Paper Potlatch Vintage Velvet
Colors Four, process
Type Latin, Ribbon
Printing Offset
Software Aldus FreeHand
Initial Print Run 5,000
Cost $2,600

Concept This poster promoted a
Christmas event connected to "El
Corazón Sangrante" ("The Bleeding
Heart"), an exhibit of traditional
and contemporary Mexican art
held at the Institute of Contemporary Art in Boston. The poster cen-
ters around a piece of art that ties
in with the name of the exhibit—a
potentially grim image. But mini-
mizing the size of the image and
using red ink for the text and a yellow pattern for the background
give the poster a festive feel.

Cost-Saving Techniques Printing
the poster at 17 by 22 inches—half
the size of many other museum
posters—helped to cut down the
cost of materials without detract-
ing from the appeal or effective-
ness of the piece. Also, Stoltze
Design donated design services,
and Aldus Press donated printing.

Distribution of Piece The piece
was posted by volunteers in public
spaces.

Response to Promotion Attendance at the event surpassed expec-
tations.

DETTER GRAPHIC DESIGN

Art Director/Studio Jeanne Detter/Detter Graphic Design
Designer/Studio Jeanne Detter/Detter Graphic Design
Photographer Harper Fritsch Studios
Client/Service Detter Graphic Design, Madison, WI/graphic design
Paper Fox River Circa Select (cover), Concrete Recycled, Centura Gloss Text (text)
Colors Six, process (body); one, match (cover)
Type Times
Printing Offset
Initial Print Run 2,000
Cost $8,238

Concept A multilayered, hand-tied cover gives this studio's miniportfolio a unique, handmade feel.
Special Visual Effect A subtle pattern of white and pale yellow for the interior background—the same as the cover pattern—gives this piece more warmth than the average glossy studio portfolio.

Cost-Saving Technique House of Type, Harper Fritsch Studios, Discover Color and Park Printing all discounted their services.
Distribution of Piece The piece was mailed throughout the year to corporate and potential clients.
Response to Promotion Comments were very positive.

MASI GRAPHICA

Art Director/Studio Eric Masi/Masi Graphica
Designer/Studio Eric Masi/Masi Graphica
Illustrator Eric Masi
Client/Service Masi Graphica, Chicago, IL/design and illustration
Paper Neenah Desert Storm Cover, Neenah Pebblestone Text
Colors Two, black and match
Type Bodega Sans Old Style
Printing Offset
Software Adobe Illustrator
Initial Print Run 1,500
Cost $1,250

Concept This tiny die-cut booklet, entitled "Better Bow Legs than No Legs!!" consists of comic illustrations of offbeat, alternative clichés. While the booklet was meant to showcase Masi's illustration work, the cleverness of the format, and its ingenuity within the confines of a limited budget, show off his design skills, too.
Special Visual Effect Variations on the trapezoid shape of the booklet are incorporated into the illustrations themselves.
Cost-Saving Techniques Design was traded for die-cutting; the paper was bought directly by the designer. The designer used a client's PMS press run to print his piece.
Distribution of Piece The piece was mailed once to designers and art directors.
Response to Promotion Response has been strong; the designer has averaged one call per week as a result, and it has landed him both design and illustration work totaling $6,500.

Art Director/Studio Robert Padovano/Robert Padovano Design

Designer/Studio Robert Padovano/Robert Padovano Design

Illustrator Robert Padovano

Client/Service Robert Padovano Design, Brooklyn, NY/graphic design

Colors Various

Type Ultra Slim (cover, inside message), Garamond (name)

Printing Ink jet printing

Software CorelDraw

Initial Print Run 30 cards, 10 boxes

Cost $30

Concept This piece could be described as a three-dimensional Christmas card. Inspired by the designer's love of Christmas seals and his desire to design his own, this piece incorporates a Christmas seal pattern on its cover. The light-bulbs on the front appear to be simply part of the pattern but turn out to be tied into the message inside, as well as to the box's surprising contents.

Cost-Saving Techniques Boxes were assembled by hand, and the design was output by the designer on an ink jet printer.

Distribution of Piece All thirty cards and ten boxes were sent to clients, with the ten boxes going to select clients.

Response to Promotion Clients were delighted, and many called the designer to thank him.

Art Director/Studio Toni
Schowalter/Schowalter 2 Design

Designers/Studio Ilene Price,
Toni Schowalter/Schowalter 2
Design

Client/Service Schowalter 2
Design, Short Hills, NJ/graphic
design

Paper Curtis Tuscan Terra, Flax
Cover

Colors Four, match

Type Lithos (heads), Kuenstler
Script (month), Futura Condensed
(text)

Printing Offset

Software QuarkXPress

Initial Print Run 3,000

Cost $6,000

Concept In lieu of a big budget,
this promotion uses archived art, a
clever concept and copy, and an
unusual format to get attention.
Using the theme "season's eatings,"
the promotion commemorates one
offbeat "holiday" per month—holidays such as Tater Day and
Macaroni Week—with a recipe
that's both workable and tongue-in-
cheek.

Special Visual Effect The calendar portion of each page is die-cut
and folded in instead of out.

Distribution of Piece The piece
was mailed at holiday time to
clients and friends.

Response to Promotion Recipients liked the piece, and one new
client can be directly connected to
it; the piece also received several
design awards, giving the studio
further publicity.

Designer/Studio Cathe Holden/Holden & Company

Clients/Services Holden & Company, Santa Rosa, CA/graphic design; ColorWise Printing & Lithography, Rancho Cordova, CA/printing

Paper French Speckletone Oatmeal

Colors Six, black and match

Type Bernhard Modern

Printing Offset

Initial Print Run 500 (200, Holden & Company; 300, ColorWise Printing)

Cost $120

Concept This joint promotion for a design firm and a printer was both a card and a small present of gift wrap and tags. Using a nondenominational theme—mistletoe—made this promotion an ideal seasonal observance for the companies' wide variety of clientele.

Special Visual Effect Silver and gold metallic inks give this piece an unclichéd holiday feel.

Special Production Technique The three colors used were double-hit for maximum effect.

Cost-Saving Techniques Design and production were traded for printing and binding with ColorWise Printing & Lithography. All artwork was produced camera-ready directly from photocopies; all package assembly was done by hand.

Distribution of Piece The piece was mailed and hand-delivered to clients, vendors and friends.

Response to Promotion The piece garnered the design firm recognition in local design competition and warm appreciation from clients.

Designer/Studio Cathe Holden/ Holden & Company

Client/Service Holden & Company, Santa Rosa, CA/ graphic design; ColorWise Printing & Lithography, Rancho Cordova, CA/printing

Paper Neenah Classic Crest Avon Brilliant White

Colors Six, black and match

Type Yale, Bordeaux Roman

Printing Offset

Software Adobe Illustrator

Initial Print Run 500 (200, Holden & Company; 300, ColorWise Printing)

Cost $450

Concept This piece builds on the mistletoe piece from the previous year, this time using another fairly nondenominational motif, a deer. Again using the concept of being both a card and a present of gift wrap and tags, this piece conveys thoughtfulness and goodwill toward its recipients.

Special Production Technique The die from the previous year's promotion was reused for this piece's die-cut envelope.

Cost-Saving Techniques Design and production were traded for printing and binding services, with paper costs divided between Holden & Company and ColorWise Printing. Clip art was used for the illustrations.

Distribution of Piece The piece was mailed and hand-delivered to clients, vendors and friends.

SEASONAL
PROMOTIONAL PIECES

Art Director/Studio Steve Curry/ Curry Design, Inc.

Designers/Studio Steve Curry, Jason Scheideman/Curry Design, Inc.

Illustrators Steve Curry, Angela Shin

Client/Service Skil-Set Graphix, Los Angeles, CA/service bureau and silkscreening

Paper Crack-and-peel labels

Colors Four to six, black and match

Type Various

Printing Silkscreening

Software Aldus FreeHand, QuarkXPress

Initial Print Run 500 to 1,000 per label

Cost $1,000 to $1,500 per label

Concept This promotion—one that has been ongoing over the past two years—consists of seasonal labels put on job bags from Skil-Set Graphix. About ten different labels are used each year, with the only common elements among them being their commemoration of a holiday, their demonstration of expert silkscreening, and their incorporation of Skil-Set's name and phone number.

Special Visual Effects Spot varnishes, metallic inks, and a wide variety of other special effects show off Skil-Set's capabilities.

Response to Promotion The promotional campaign has acquired a following: Clients now anticipate the arrival of a different label on their job bag.

LAMBERT DESIGN STUDIO

Art Director/Studio Christie Lambert/Lambert Design Studio
Designers/Studio Christie Lambert, Joy Cathey/Lambert Design Studio
Illustrators Christie Lambert, Joy Cathey
Copywriter Joy Jennings Renfro
Client/Service Lambert Design Studio, Dallas, TX/graphic design
Paper Mac Tac label stock
Colors Two, match
Type Matrix Narrow, hand-lettering
Printing Offset
Software Applescan, Adobe Illustrator
Initial Print Run 400
Cost $1,366

Concept This New Year's promotion is based on the Southern tradition of eating black-eyed peas on New Year's Day for good luck. The fact that it was sent for New Year's rather than Christmas helped the studio's piece stand out from other studios' seasonal pieces. To inject some intrigue into the mailing, the studio used the name "Lucky P Ranch" on the return address of the piece. Clever, pun-filled copy—including a mock ode to the pea—made this promotion a keeper, and the recipe on the back makes this promotion useful, too.

Special Visual Effects The box and the package design reinforce one another, and the red and green highlights are far from the clichéd holiday reds and greens.

Distribution of Piece The piece was mass-mailed once primarily to prospects, but also to clients and studio friends.

Response to Promotion Many of the prospects remembered and kept the peas, giving the studio an identity when it did follow-up calls.

Art Director/Studio Jack Anderson/Hornall Anderson Design Works
Designers/Studio Jack Anderson, Mary Hermes/Hornall Anderson Design Works
Photographer Darrell Peterson
Letterer George Deaver
Client/Service Food Services of America, Seattle, WA/institutional food distribution
Paper Simpson Starwhite Vicksburg
Colors Four, process, and two, match
Type Stemple Garamond
Printing Offset

Concept With its large format and upscale feel, this 19-by-26½-inch calendar stands out from the usual food service calendar. The photographic treatment of the food departs from the usual treatment of the subject, giving the photographs a glamorous, fine-art look that reinforces the high-quality image FSA wants to project. The result is a piece that is as beautiful as it is useful.
Distribution of Piece The piece was mailed and presented throughout the year to FSA customers.
Response to Promotion Recipients enjoy the calendar, and it creates a strong, positive impression of FSA.

PUSHPIN ASSOCIATES

Art Directors/Studio Seymour Chwast, William Bevington/The Pushpin Group, Inc.
Designer/Studio Gene Smith/The Pushpin Group, Inc.
Illustrator Seymour Chwast
Client/Service Pushpin Associates, New York, NY/illustrators' representative
Colors Three, black and match
Type Snell Roundhand
Printing Offset
Software QuarkXPress
Initial Print Run 200

Concept This illustrated bouquet of flowers was delivered to clients on Valentine's Day, with an invitation to a luncheon. The format ensured that recipients would open and read the invitation; sending a poster of flowers, instead of real ones, made this a promotion clients could keep and enjoy for years to come. The poster is also particular-

ly suited to promoting Pushpin's illustration.
Distribution of Piece The piece was delivered by messenger once to clients and prospective clients.
Response to Promotion The luncheon was well-attended.

EVENSON DESIGN GROUP

Art Director/Studio Stan Evenson/Evenson Design Group
Designer/Studio Stan Evenson/Evenson Design Group
Client/Service Evenson Design Group, Culver City, CA/graphic design
Paper French Speckletone
Colors Three, black and match
Type Caslon 540
Printing Offset
Software QuarkXPress
Initial Print Run 500

Concept In lieu of a traditional holiday gift, Evenson Design Group sent its clients a gift they could really use: a copy of *The Popcorn Report* by Faith Popcorn. The book predicts coming trends in society and how these trends will impact the business world. The theme is a useful one for the studio's corporate clientele, as well as a fitting commemoration of a new year. The studio designed a special box and book jacket for the occasion; the interior jacket flap explains the importance of the book and includes Stan Evenson's holiday greetings.
Special Visual Effect The script type treatment of the word *Popcorn* is repeated in initial form on the front cover.
Distribution of Piece The piece was mailed during the holiday season and occasionally throughout the year to new and existing clients.
Response to Promotion Recipients loved the promotion.

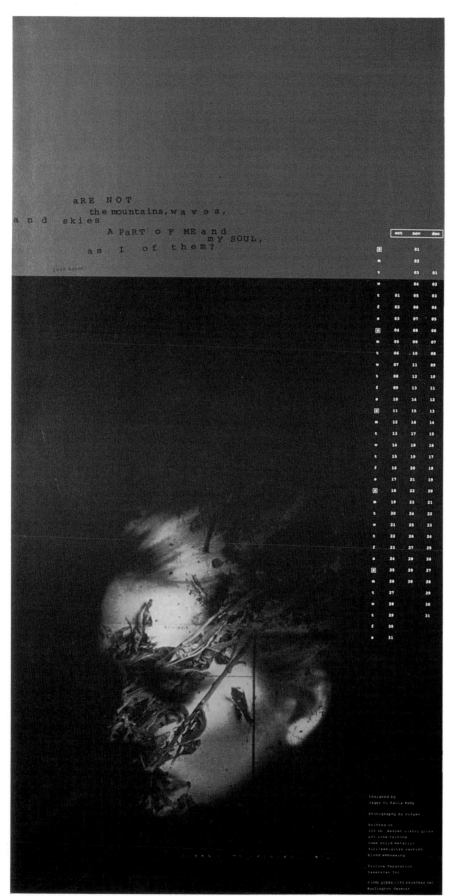

Art Director/Studio Janet Johnson/Jager DiPaola Kemp Design
Creative Director/Studio Michael Jager/Jager DiPaola Kemp Design
Designer/Studio Janet Johnson/Jager DiPaola Kemp Design
Photographer Eric Dinyer
Client/Service Queen City Printers, Burlington, VT/printing
Paper Warren Lustro Gloss
Colors Four, match, plus varnish
Type Courier, Bank Gothic
Printing Offset
Software Aldus PageMaker
Initial Print Run 3,000

Concept This fall poster/calendar promotion for a printer uses an intriguing visual that merges an image of humanity with images of nature. Printing a tritone over a solid metallic silver background gives this poster visual depth and gives the printer a chance to demonstrate his expertise. The overall effect of this image and color scheme is a sense of mystery that is appropriate to the autumnal theme of the poster, without resorting to a hackneyed fall color scheme.

Special Visual Effect The name of Queen City Printers is blind-embossed at the bottom of the poster in the same Courier type-face used for most of the poster's text.

Distribution of Piece Queen City Printers mailed the piece once to clients and potential clients.

BUTLER PAPER AND
LITHOGRAPHIX, INC.

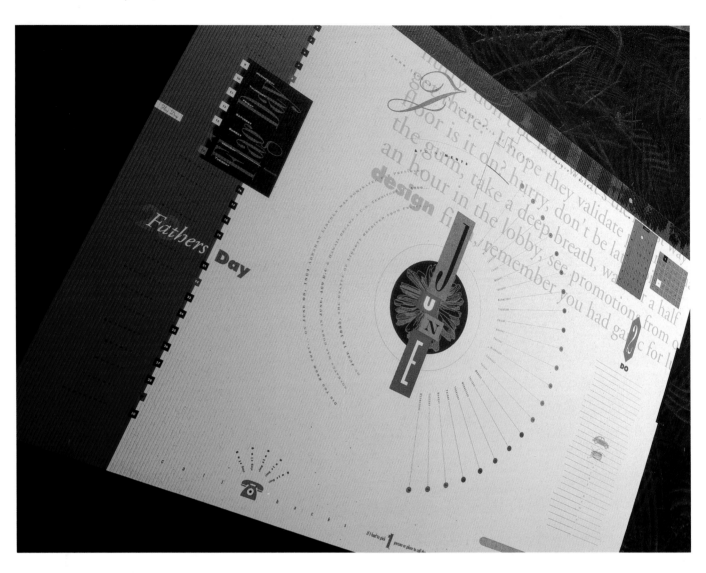

Art Director/Studio Steve
Curry/Curry Design, Inc.
Designer/Studio Jason
Scheideman/Curry Design, Inc.
Clients/Services Lithographix,
Inc., Los Angeles, CA/printer;
Butler Paper/paper supplier
Paper Beckett Ridge Ash
Colors Six, black and match
Type Bank Gothic, Engravers,
Adobe Garamond, Copperplate,
Ribbon, Trade Gothic Bold
Condensed 20, Odeon, Kuenstler

Script
Printing Offset
Software Aldus FreeHand
Initial Print Run 20,000
Cost None (design donated)

Concept Butler Paper commissioned a series of calendar posters,
done by a wide variety of design
firms, to jointly promote its paper
and Lithographix's printing abilities. Studios were required to use
Butler paper but otherwise were

allowed a great deal of artistic freedom—freedom Curry Design, Inc.,
used appealingly to create this
poster for June. While this calendar
contains all the information the
average calendar page contains—
including minicalendars of the previous and the next months,
acknowledgment of holidays, and
space to write daily activities for
the month—these features are
incorporated in surprising ways.
Special Visual Effects The layers

of various typefaces, the six ink colors, and a few small, whimsical
illustrations combine to create a
piece that will still hold some sur-
prises for the viewer after a month
of viewing.
Distribution of Piece The piece
was mailed and hand-delivered
once to Lithographix and Butler
clients.

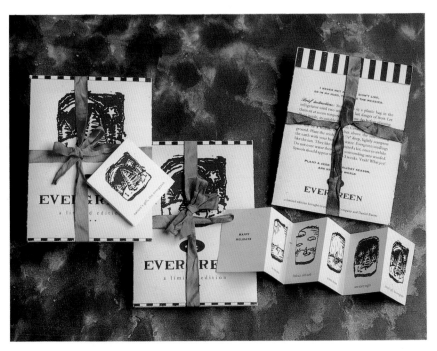

Art Director/Studio Carol Neiley/I & Company

Designer/Studio Carol Neiley/I & Company

Illustrator Daniel Baxter

Clients/Services I & Company, Red Hook, NY/graphic design; Daniel Baxter Illustration, Red Hook, NY/illustration

Paper Cross Pointe Genesis Milkweed and Husk

Colors One, black

Type Centaur, Copperplate, Englische Schreibschrift

Printing Laser printing

Software Aldus PageMaker, Adobe Photoshop

Initial Print Run 200

Cost $400

Concept A longing brought about by treeless New York City inspired this seasonal promotion. The hang-tag depicts the evolution of an evergreen from seed to full-grown tree; the seeds inside allow recipients to grow their own trees. This promotion is seasonally appropriate yet nondenominational, environmentally aware yet not preachy.

Special Visual Effects The addition of a colored ribbon accent brightens this one-color piece economically.

Cost-Saving Techniques The packages were laser printed, hand-assembled and tied, and hand-delivered.

Art Director/Studio Carol Neiley/I & Company

Designer/Studio Carol Neiley/I & Company

Illustrator Daniel Baxter

Clients/Services I & Company, Red Hook, NY/graphic design; Daniel Baxter Illustration, Red Hook, NY/illustration

Paper Handmade

Colors One, black

Type Centaur, hand-lettering

Printing Laser printing

Software Aldus PageMaker, Adobe Photoshop

Initial Print Run 200

Cost $1,600

Concept This autumn promotion, a gift of a macrame bag that was designed to discourage the use of nonrecyclable plastic grocery bags, was a natural follow-up to the previous year's Christmas 4-Evergreen seed promotion.

Special Visual Effect Using the same kind of faux-antique grosgrain ribbon to affix the hang-tag also visually ties this promotion to the earlier 4-Evergreen seed promotion.

Cost-Saving Techniques Vibrantly inked rubber stamps, custom-made from Daniel Baxter's illustrations, add color to the mailing tube at minimal cost; laser printing of the hang-tag, hand-assembly, and hand-delivery also helped to keep costs down.

CURRY DESIGN, INC.

Art Director/Studio Steve Curry/Curry Design, Inc.
Designer/Studio Steve Curry/Curry Design, Inc.
Illustrator Steve Curry/Curry Design, Inc.
Client/Service Curry Design, Inc., Venice, CA/graphic design
Paper French Speckletone, kraft cardboard
Colors Five, black and match
Type Linoscript, Garamond, Futura
Printing Silkscreening
Software Aldus FreeHand
Initial Print Run 500
Cost $15,000

Concept This holiday gift from Curry Design, an always welcome bottle of wine, serves its purpose of spreading good feeling about the studio. The wine label and box use a traditional color palette of red, green and metallic silver; these are combined with tan and black for a less-than-traditional effect. The "peace on earth" message is appropriately nondenominational.

Special Visual Effect The words *peace on earth* and *goodwill towards all* are enlarged, printed with silver metallic ink, and used as a background pattern on the box.

Cost-Saving Techniques Skil-Set Graphix traded silkscreening services for the studio's design services.

Distribution of Piece The piece was mailed and hand-delivered during the holiday season to clients and friends.

Response to Promotion This promotion brought the studio three new referrals.

Art Directors/Studio Kristen and Omid Balouch/Zubi Design
Client/Service Boxart, Inc., Brooklyn, NY/fine art crating and packing
Type Hand-lettering
Printing Silkscreening
Software Aldus FreeHand
Initial Print Run 70
Cost $8,500

Concept This seasonal gift from a company that crates and packs fine art playfully interprets the company's name with a minicrate of alphabet blocks. The blocks give the promotion a childlike feel appropriate for the Christmas season, but the execution of the concept—with each letter interpreted differently on each side of each block—shows an attention to detail that's anything but childlike. The result is a soft-sell promotion that appeals to the company's artistic clientele in charming, yet effective, fashion.

Distribution of Piece The piece was mailed once to clients and potential clients.

Art Director/Studio John White/White Design

Designers/Studio John White, Susan Garland/White Design

Photographer Russ Widstrand

Illustrators Kevin Newman, Dennis Mukai/Flatland; Susan Garland, Aram Youssefian, Carlos Delgado, Jonathan Lund, Roger Xavier, Rik Olson

Client/Service White Design, Long Beach, CA/graphic design

Paper Champion Kromekote (cards), UV Ultra 2 Columns (wrapper)

Colors Three, match, and one, process

Type Garamond, Futura

Printing Lithography

Software QuarkXPress, Adobe Illustrator

Initial Print Run 500

Cost $3,809 (printing donated)

Concept This set of nine Christmas cards promoted the work of White Design, as well as the work of nine photographers and illustrators with whom the studio had worked in the previous year. Sending nine blank cards to each client, to be sent out to their own clients and friends, increased the promotion's potential audience ninefold, at no additional cost to the studio. With this in mind, the photographer, illustrators and studio were credited on the back of each card, so recipients would know whom to contact if they wanted to see more work.

Special Visual Effects Metallic green, red and gold inks give an appropriately festive feel to the cards; the red oval on the wrapper's band features a subtly reversed-out version of the studio's logo and is surrounded by a border incorporat-ing the studio's name.

Cost-Saving Technique All illus-tration, photography and printing were donated in return for a credit line on the cards and for finished samples.

Distribution of Piece Packets were mailed to clients and suppli-ers during the Christmas season.

Response to Promotion The stu-dio got an overwhelmingly positive response to the promotion, and many suggested that the studio try marketing the cards; they're cur-rently pursuing this.

Art Director/Studio Jeanne Detter/Detter Graphic Design

Designers/Studio Jeanne Detter, Michele Rayome, Tammy Kosbau/Detter Graphic Design

Client/Service Detter Graphic Design, Madison, WI/graphic design

Paper Frostbrite Coated Matte Cover by Consolidated (notecards); Neenah Classic Crest (envelopes); corrugated slate from Vicki Schober Company, Inc. (boxes)

Colors Two, match

Type Various

Printing Offset

Initial Print Run 25 each of 17 versions; 150 each of Christmas card

Cost $6,683

Concept Detter Graphic Design targeted just seventeen clients for this personalized promotion; these clients got twenty-five notecards, designed especially for them and incorporating their name in the design, as a Christmas present from the studio. The piece was a great way for the studio to demonstrate its design skills, and to give clients a present that was both lovely and useful.

Special Visual Effect The package of cards came wrapped in corrugated paper, held together by a band saying "You are unique," which fastened with Velcro.

Special Production Technique All seventeen versions were printed on the same press sheet.

Cost-Saving Technique Using screen tints gave the designers variety to choose from, while holding costs down.

Distribution of Piece The piece was mailed to clients at Christmastime.

Response to Promotion Clients were impressed, and they thanked the studio.

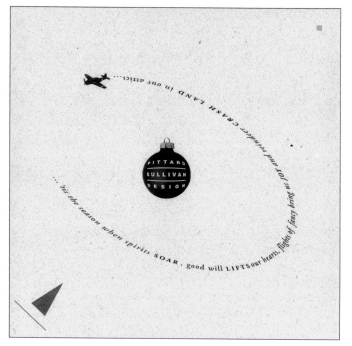

Art Director/Studio Flavio Kampah/Pittard Sullivan Design
Designers/Studio Flavio Kampah, Bill Dawson/Pittard Sullivan Design
Macintosh Producer Mark Plumkett
Client/Service Pittard Sullivan Design, Venice, CA/broadcast design
Paper Neenah Paper Recycled
Colors Three, black and match
Type Copperplate, Helvetica, Bodoni
Printing Offset
Software Adobe Illustrator, Adobe Photoshop
Initial Print Run 1,000
Cost $9,000

Concept Merging two female portraits done in different styles, and overlaying that with various seasonal greetings done in a wide range of type treatments, suggests this design firm's breadth of styles, as well as its skill at combining these styles.

Special Visual Effects An unusual gatefold format, and red and green tints that are slightly off-center from the traditional seasonal hues, make this card stand out from the usual run of Christmas cards. The circular type treatment used in the interior also commands attention.

Distribution of Piece The piece was mailed to clients and potential clients.

Art Director/Studio Steve Curry/ Curry Design, Inc.

Designers/Studio Steve Curry, Erica Buchanon/Curry Design, Inc.

Illustrator Erica Buchanon

Client/Service E! Entertainment Television, Los Angeles, CA/television network

Paper French Speckletone Black

Colors Three, match

Printing Silkscreening

Software Aldus FreeHand

Initial Print Run 2,000

Cost $10,000

Concept This E! Entertainment Television mug was a holiday gift for E!'s affiliate networks. The "peace on earth" theme was appropriately nondenominational; the casual, lighthearted style of the new network is reflected in the style of the illustrations used on the mug.

Special Visual Effects The combination of gold and bronze metallic inks gives the mug a festive yet unclichéd seasonal look.

Distribution of Piece The piece was mailed to E!'s affiliate networks.

COPYRIGHT NOTICES AND PHOTOGRAPHY CREDITS

Only the names and addresses of individuals or studios who entered their work in this competition are included in this directory; to reach illustrators, photographers, or design studios who are listed in the project credits but who are not listed here, please contact the studio with whom they collaborated.

246 Fifth Design
246 Fifth Ave.
Ottawa, Ontario K1S 2N3
Canada

After Hours
1201 East Jefferson
Phoenix, AZ 85034

Bernhardt Fudyma Design Group
133 East 36th Street
New York, NY 10016

Bill Mayer Inc.
240 Forkner Drive
Decatur, GA 30030

Boelts Bros. Design
14 East Second Street
Tucson, AZ 85705

Carolyn Fisher Illustration
473 Columbus Ave. 1 D
New York, NY 10024

Chermayeff & Geismar Inc.
15 East 26th Street
New York, NY 10010

Joe Ciardiello
2182 Clove Road
Staten Island, NY 10305

Clement Mok designs, Inc.
600 Townsend Street, Penthouse
San Francisco, CA 94103

Curry Design
1501 Main Street
Venice, CA 90291

Daniel Baxter Illustration
RR3, Box 15, Feller Newmark Road
Red Hook, NY 12571

Darrel Kolosta, Illustrator
4150 Park Blvd.
Oakland, CA 94602

Detter Graphic Design
4222 Milwaukee Street, Suite 17
Madison, WI 53714

Dynamic Duo
95 Kings Highway, South
Westport, CT 06880

Evenson Design Group
4445 Overland Ave.
Culver City, CA 90230

Firehouse 101 Design
492 Armstrong Street
Columbus, OH 43215

Focus 2
2105 Commerce St., #102
Dallas, TX 75201

Full Circle Advertising & Design
218 Parkwood Ave.
Kenmore, NY 14217-2833

Grafik Communications, Ltd.
1199 North Fairfax Street, Suite 700
Alexandria, VA 22314

Gunnar Swanson Design Office
739 Indiana Ave.
Venice, CA 90291-2728

Holden & Co.
804 College Ave.
Santa Rosa, CA 95404

Hornall Anderson Design Works
1008 Western Ave., #600
Seattle, WA 98104

Jager DiPaola Kemp Design
308 Pine Street
Burlington, VT 05401

James Leung Design NY
455 84th Street
Brooklyn, NY 11209

Jock McDonald Photography
46 Gilbert Street
San Francisco, CA 94103

John Payne Photography Ltd.
2250 West Grand Ave.
Chicago, IL 60612

Joined at the Hip
859 Sandcastle Drive
Cardiff, CA 92007

Julia Tam Design
2216 Via La Brea
Palos Verdes, CA 90274

Juliette Borda Illustration
416 Clinton Street
Brooklyn, NY 11231

Kampah Visions
2313 Frey Ave.
Venice, CA 90291

Lambert Design Studio
7007 Twin Hills, Suite 213
Dallas, TX 75231

Masi Graphica
4244 North Bell
Chicago, IL 60618

Matthews Illustration
7528 Ethel Ave.
St. Louis, MO 63117

Maureen Erbe Design
1948 South La Cienega Blvd.
Los Angeles, CA 90034

Maverick Art Tribe
112 C 17th Ave. NW
Calgary, Alberta T2M 0M6
Canada

Mercier-Wimberg Photography
8751 West Washington Blvd.
Culver City, CA 90232

Midnight Oil Studios
51 Melcher Street
Boston, MA 02210

Modern Dog
601 Valley Street, #309
Seattle, WA 98109

Pace Studios
665 Third Street, #250
San Francisco, CA 94107

Patrick Barta Photography
80 South Washington Street, #204
Seattle, WA 98104

Pentagram Design
620 Davis Street
San Francisco, CA 94610

Peterson & Company
2200 North Lamar S-310
Dallas, TX 75202

The Pushpin Group, Inc.
215 Park Avenue South, Floor 13
New York, NY 10003

Richard Prahm Design
1456 Vallejo Street, #205
San Francisco, CA 94109

Rickabaugh Graphics
384 West Johnstown Road
Gahanna, OH 43230

The Riordon Design Group
1001 Queen Street West
Mississauga, Ontario L5H 4E1
Canada

Robert Padovano Design
538 82nd Street
Brooklyn, NY 11209

Irena Roman
P.O. Box 571
369 Clapp Road
Scituate, MA 02066

Sayles Graphic Design
308 Eighth Street
Des Moines, IA 50309

Schowalter 2 Design
21 The Crescent
Short Hills, NJ 07078

Scott Hull Associates
68 East Franklin Street
Dayton, OH 45459

Segura Inc.
540 North Lake Shore Drive #324
Chicago, IL 60611-3431

Shannon Designs
3536 Edmund Blvd.
Minneapolis, MN 55406

Steelhaus Design
4991 Eller Road
Chattanooga, TN 37416-1820

Stephen Alcorn Design
112 West Main Street
Cambridge, NY 12816

Stephen Schudlich Illustration + Design
1755 Livernois
Troy, MI 48083

Stewart Monderer Design, Inc.
10 Thacher Street, Suite 112
Boston, MA 02113

Stoltze Design
49 Melcher Ave.
Boston, MA 02210

Studio Wilks
8800 Venice Blvd.
Los Angeles, CA 90034

Tharp Did It
50 University Ave.
Los Gatos, CA 95030

Timbuk 2 Design
2475 Euclid Crescent
Upland, CA 91784

Vaughn Wedeen Creative
407 Rio Grande NW
Albuquerque, NM 87104

Webster Design Associates
5060 Dodge Street
Omaha, NE 68132

White Design
4500 East Pacific Coast
Long Beach, CA 90804

William Reuter Design
657 Bryant Street
San Francisco, CA 94107

Zeewy Design
111 Forrest Ave., #2
Narberth, PA 19072

Zubi Design
57 Norman Ave.
Brooklyn, NY 11222

INDEX OF DESIGN FIRMS

INDEX OF CLIENTS

INDEX OF COLLATERAL